Mud, Guts & Glory

Tips & Training for
Extreme Obstacle Racing

Mark Hatmaker
with Doug Werner

Tracks Publishing
San Diego, California

Mud, Guts & Glory
Tips & Training for Extreme Obstacle Racing
Mark Hatmaker with **Doug Werner**

Tracks Publishing
140 Brightwood Avenue
Chula Vista, CA 91910
619-476-7125
tracks@cox.net
www.startupsports.com
trackspublishing.com

Copyright © 2013 by Mark Hatmaker and Doug Werner
10 9 8 7 6 5 4 3 2 1

Publisher's Cataloging-in-Publication

Hatmaker, Mark.

Mud, guts & glory : tips & training for extreme obstacle racing / Mark Hatmaker
; with Doug Werner. -- San Diego, Calif. : Tracks Pub., c20

p. ; cm.
ISBN: 978-1-935937-56-2
Includes index.
     Summary: Obstacle racing is a grueling physical challenge, where competitors test their mettle against obstacles, terrain, and conditioning similar to military boot camps. This book provides an in-depth look at the training, conditioning, gear, preparation, tactics, and logistics for making it through climbing mud-covered ropes, fording swamps, mounting walls, executing an effective belly-crawl, and numerous other tips for the wild chaos that might ensue, plus the ever-present problem of cleaning up. Whether racing for fun or in it to win it, Mud, Guts & Glory is the one-stop guide for enduring the race from start to finish. --Publisher.

     1. Obstacle racing. 2. Obstacle racing--Training. 3. Extreme
     sports. 4. Physical fitness.
I. Werner, Doug, 1950- II. Title.

GV749.7 .H38 2013   2013940730
796.04/6--dc23

Books by Mark Hatmaker

No Holds Barred Fighting:
The Ultimate Guide to Submission Wrestling

More No Holds Barred Fighting:
Killer Submissions

No Holds Barred Fighting:
Savage Strikes

No Holds Barred Fighting:
Takedowns

No Holds Barred Fighting:
The Clinch

No Holds Barred Fighting:
The Ultimate Guide to Conditioning

No Holds Barred Fighting:
The Kicking Bible

No Holds Barred Fighting:
The Book of Essential Submissions

Boxing Mastery

No Second Chance:
A Reality-Based Guide to Self-Defense

MMA Mastery:
Flow Chain Drilling and Integrated O/D Training

MMA Mastery:
Ground and Pound

MMA Mastery:
Strike Combinations

Boxer's Book of Conditioning & Drilling

Boxer's Bible of Counterpunching

Books are available through major bookstores
and booksellers on the Internet.

TO THE BONA FIDE HEROS
who fill the rosters of the
world's Elite Special Forces,
who train for life and death
scenarios using many of the
elements found in obstacle
course racing. We pampered
civilians know beyond the
shadow of a doubt that we are
only big kids playing "Let's
pretend" in your deadly
serious sandbox.

Thanks for the jobs you do.

Acknowledgments
Phyllis Carter
Kylie Hatmaker
Mitch Thomas
Shane Tucker

Contents

In recent years obstacle course racing has taken the world in its big muddy arms and shown us that middle way where *we can test not only our endurance and not only our strength, but dozens of other attributes* you didn't even know you wanted to flex.

Introduction

So you've had that gym membership for a while, you're fit, feeling pretty good about yourself and you'd like to take this brand-new body out for a test drive and see what she'll do. Maybe at first you sign up for one of the myriad local 5Ks, but after reaping more than a few participant T-shirts, you begin finding the 3.2 miles on man-made roads a bit less than compelling or challenging.

Where do you go next to get that little jolt of challenge juice that you felt in your first race? Do you decide to up the distance — sign up for a 10K or a marathon? Do we go all mondo-serious, shave our body hair and see what this Ironman thing is all about?

These are all good options, but we gotta admit, they are a bit one-sided. They are all endurance oriented events that tend to skew toward whippet lean folks in the upper ranks. Maybe you start to recognize that your gym has these things called free weights and pull-up bars and kettlebells and other such toys that are singing their siren song and causing you to lose attention in the repetitiveness of the laps on the track or the pretend miles in spin class. What are these strength building toys all about?

You've built a body that is looking respectably beach-ready with a bit of buff tone here and there. You've found out that if you turn just right in the mirror you can find that muscle in your back just like Hugh Jackman has in that Wolverine movie. Now that you've got this brand-new bikini/board shorts sporting body, what do you do with it beyond walk it proud at the local beach or pool (and hit the odd flex or two every time you pass a reflective surface)?

Sure, you've gotten stronger, but maybe not strong in the same class as your local power lifting club, so competing here is not necessarily an option. You've gotten more toned, but let's face it, you're no match for the pharmaceutical perfection of your local body building contestants. I mean, come on, some of these power lifters and body builders are huge hunks of human beings.

Conundrum, huh? We've got rail thin greyhounds in one area of competitive fun and big Brahma bulls in the other. What's the respectably fit human being who has taken the time not to specialize, but to be prepared for a variety of physical challenges to do? Methinks that unless you've blindly picked up this book and paid zero attention to the cover or title you already know the answer to that one.

In recent years obstacle course racing has taken the world in its big muddy arms and shown us that middle way where we can test not only our endurance and not only our strength, but dozens of other attributes you didn't even know you wanted to flex. You get to test your agility, your stamina, your flexibility (both physical and mental), your determination, your teamwork, your problem solving skills, and at the end of the race, your laundry prowess.

This book is meant to be your go-to manual for how to get the most out of this muddy middle way. We'll be talking race tips, obstacle tactics, race specific conditioning and pre- and post-race logistics to streamline your experience. In short, this manual is meant to be your how-to-get-started if you've never run one and your how-to-do-it-better if you've run a dozen.

What's the dirt on the soap opera?

If you've been paying a bit of attention to the obstacle course racing phenomenon over the past couple of years, you may be privy to the behind-the-scenes machinations engaged in by some of the event promoters. There's a whole lot of "He said this" and "I was first" and "They stole this" and "Oh, yeah, well they stole that" yakkity-yak going on. To be frank, there's been a fair amount of Machiavellian legal wrangling and some suspect business ethics engaged in by a few.

Would you like the skinny on all this stuff? Well, you're not going to find it in this book for two reasons.

First, to be blunt, what's going on, or has gone on among some of these folks is none of your business. Don't take offense; it's none of my business either. It's the business of the folks involved — nobody else's. I'm not an idiot and I know I am hiding nothing from you. If you're a busy-body you're going to Google it or Bing it. Then you will have all the gossip, and your life will be so much the better for knowing who called who a poopy-pants.

Second, these events are F-U-N. I really don't see why I should muddy my opinion about my own subjective state of having more doses of fun by meddling, gossiping or picking sides in affairs that have nothing whatsoever to do with me.

You know the old rule — if you can't say anything nice, keep your mouth shut. The good news is I've got plenty of nice things to say about these events so there's no need to spend any more time on the negative.

What it is and what it ain't
Before we go whole hog and leap feet first into muddy water up to our chest so we can crawl up a slick embankment on the other side, we should get some definitions out of the way. That is, we need to state just what this book is about.

Is it about mud racing?
Is it about adventure racing?
Is it about obstacle course racing?

There is a common tendency to confuse what are actually three separate classes of event. It's an easy mistake to make. After all, if you look at an obstacle course competitor you see someone who did indeed race through mud and have a bit of adventure, so are we just splitting hairs? Not really. Here are the distinctions.

Mud racing

Mud races are races that feature mud. How's that for a definition? I'm not being facetious. Mud racing, to the initiated, refers to any race that contains no obstacle element beyond the mud itself (usually in a pit or bog), and the object is to run or bike the course as rapidly as possible. Again, the main distinction being the lack of obstacles outside of the mud.

Adventure racing

Adventure racing is easier to distinguish as these are typically gear-heavy events that feature long distances to be traveled via several elements. Depending on the adventure race, these elements can be trail running, mountain biking, kayaking, rappelling and other such forms of locomotion. They often feature an orienteering element which tests the competitors' map and compass skills.

Obstacle course racing

These races are all about the obstacle, or more to the point, testing how well you navigate and handle obstruction. Obstacles can be natural (a river to swim, a swamp to muck through, a muddy bank to slither up) or man-made (cargo nets to climb, walls to get over, barbed wire to crawl under).

Obstacle races are often all about prepositions — you've got to go under, over, through, on top and between a variety of barriers. You never go around them.

Well, you can go around them if you want to, but come on, who wants to go around the obstacles? If you sign up for an obstacle race just to go around them, then you're just trail running. If your plan is to skip or go around an obstacle, do you and me a favor, put the book down and go back to your 5Ks. You'll save yourself some time and laundry.

Is it a race or an experience?

The answer is yes to both. But that's a qualified yes on the first count. Back to that in a moment.

Participating in an obstacle course race is, indeed, an experience in both the clinical definition of the word and the emotional "Man, was that a blast or what!" sense of the word. There is an undeniable visceral thrill each time you encounter an obstacle and each time you successfully navigate that obstacle.

When you first round that switchback on the trail and discover that you are expected to wade waist deep through mud to get to a muddy 20-foot rope, grasp its slick fibers, wrench yourself from the sucking mud holding your legs fast, climb to the top and ring the bell — your first visceral flutter is "Shit, can I even do this?" Then if/when you ring that bell and come off the rope, visceral thrill #2 hits and you think to yourself, "Shit! I just did that!"

That feeling is golden, my friends.

You can keep chunking "Man, that was awesome!" points into the experience column with every obstacle you encounter, every bonding experience you enjoy on the course and every "And then this happened ..." story you get to tell over a beer after the race is run.

Obstacle course races/events are indeed an experience and, yes, they can be a race in some aspects — sometimes.

Here's that qualified part I mentioned before.

Most of these events offer a timing chip so that you check your time post-race "to see how you did." In my opinion, you know how you did while you're doing it — that's how you did. But if you're all about pinning your very own personal state of mind on something outside yourself, by all means check your time to see where you stand in the muddy hierarchy. I must admit I have a few reservations regarding the efficacy of the "Here's how I did" aspect of some of these events. These reservations stand outside of my own "Just have a blast!" approach because I have never once in the dozens of these events I've run, checked my time.

> *I've always known what my time was — I had a good time. That's good enough for me.*

I've always known what my time was — I had a good time. That's good enough for me. But beyond my own opinion, here are my objective reasons to arch an eyebrow when the conversation turns to competitive time stories.

Numero uno — I'm not sure the chips all stand up to the mud, or if there isn't sometimes a bit of human error on the organizational side of things. You see, I may never check my time, but wife, Kylie, who has run all of these races with me (she's the good looking one in the photos) does check. I simply ask not to be informed of the times. I live by the rule that ignorance usually is bliss.

She reports that for approximately every three events we participate in (large brand name events or local concoctions), we have no time recorded whatsoever or we have incorrect times posted compared with her watch.

The timing errors have gone both ways making us much faster in some cases and much slower in others. In one case, our times varied between each other by seven minutes. I mention this because we have crossed every finish line side-by-side. In another case, we apparently ran a heat so quickly that we finished 30 minutes before we started.

An additional concern I have in cases where we assume all timing chips function at their optimum, is just what are we measuring here? Simply running the course time? Or do we factor in the obstacles? I ask because I have yet to run a single race where I did not see an approximate skip-the-obstacle rate of ten percent. That is, some of these jack-rabbit fast folks may be touting a trail running time that you simply can't beat because you actually took the time to take two shots at that 10-foot wall.

We've also got to consider bottlenecking. No matter how well a course is designed or superbly organized, you will inevitably encounter human traffic jams as you and dozens of muddy folks stand in line (sometimes for 15-20 minutes) to hit that oh, so cool zip line or Burma bridge.

You also have to consider changes in the course while the course is in operation. Case in point, I once stood in line for a zip (only one was available) to cross a two-acre lake — so we had a bottleneck to begin with. My wife and I were finally about spots six and seven to ride the line when the cable broke. Now it's decision time. A course that previously had zero swimming now has a great deal of swimming. How do those times compare to those who swam and those who skipped that bit of fatigue. (I forgot to mention this was C-O-L-D water, and swimming in cold water is one energy-sucking activity).

There is also, to be frank, an integrity issue to be accounted for. Some events, such as the very well run Spartan Race events, impose a 30-burpee penalty for those who fail or opt to skip an obstacle. Personally, I love this rule — feels like extra skin in the game, so to speak. But of the many Spartans I've run (several Sprints, a few Supers and Beasts to this point) I can count on the fingers of two hands the individuals who were performing the burpees to the standard required or the folks who actually did the full required 30.

If you run a Spartan (and I highly recommend that you do) there are opportunities for burpees left and right. More often than not you see some pretty weak sauce passing for a burpee, or a vague half-hearted 5-6 repetitions followed by a casually furtive look around to see whose watching and then back to the course. So tell me, how does the honest runners' time compete with this bit of Lance Armstrong-ish behavior?

There is another time killer to be encountered on the course, and this is one to be grateful for. Some folks who are giving an honest shot at each and every obstacle require a hand (there are some obstacles out there where teamwork is the only way to navigate them). I love to lend a hand. One of my best memories in an event is stopping at a 10-foot wall and giving an assist to one person to get over the wall. One turned into two, two into three and, before I know it, my wife informs me that I have spent approximately 10 minutes side-by-side with a Marine whose name I never knew giving a leg up to folks to get over that wall.

Those the nameless Marine and I helped undoubtedly sported better times than he and I did, but I wouldn't trade those moments of camaraderie among strangers for the world. That time was one of my best times.

You get the picture. Go ahead, run competitively — I have no doubt that those in the upper echelons are doing so with honor and fleet skill. But you'll forgive me if the vast majority of the talk of times strikes me as a little less than valuable or interesting.

Competitive vs. cooperative mindset

Lest anyone think from the previous section that I'm against running an obstacle race for all you're worth, or con showing up with an "in it to win it" attitude —

naw, not at all. Just wanted to provide a little perspective about the intangible obstacles that you may not have considered that can affect your time or performance. With that said there are two broad general ways to approach an obstacle course event.

The first is, of course, to do as well as possible. That is, reaping the fastest time you can while navigating each and every obstacle and performing all penalties to the competition standard. To strive for anything less would be cheating, and mighty revealing of character.

The second approach is to do as well as you possibly can. That is, reaping the fastest time you can while navigating each and every obstacle and performing all penalties to the competition standard. To strive for anything less would be cheating, and mighty revealing of character.

Huh? That's practically the same paragraph isn't it? Wanting to do well whether you are playing competitively or cooperatively is a given. Both classes of folks have good performance at the heart of their motivation. I mean, who signs up for something to half-ass it? (Well, maybe those with the integrity deficits we mentioned earlier.)

What will usually distinguish the competitive and the cooperative mindset will be numbers on the team, or more specifically, the idea of a team itself. If a good time in the chronological sense is more important than a good time in the bonding sense, then you've got to be prepared to leave folks behind, or skip the bit where you assist strangers.

If you're in it to win it, it might be best to skip forming a team altogether. Inevitably, there will be folks on a team who lack a certain agility or ability to cope with this or that obstacle (that person might even be you). If you are likely to take a dim view of having to stop and assist, or at least cheer and encourage a lagging teammate under the barbed wire, or get him

These events are ideal for building teamwork and camaraderie.

through his third set of penalty burpees, then you might want to designate yourself as a solo runner.

Keep in mind that "team" may be folks you accumulate as you move through the course. I have met many fine folks because we rendezvoused at more than one obstacle and sort of fell in together. Once you do this, a kind of "leave no man behind" mentality spontaneously rears its head, and you find yourself personally invested in the performance of people whom you've never laid eyes on before and may never again — like the nameless Marine.

I have run every event with my wife either right by my side or at least within sight. She and I use a rule that if one is taking a recovery pace, the other, if they choose, can sprint ahead, and we will rendezvous at the next obstacle. I have run with numerous friends, family members, folks I met before the race started and folks I met during the race. These events are ideal for building teamwork and camaraderie.

I have also "run" numerous events with my brother-in-law Shane Tucker. The word "run" is in scare quotes because Shane is one of those jack-rabbit fast guys I mentioned earlier. He runs competitively in road events throughout the year and, although we may travel to a few races together and bunk together and start the race together, he and I both know that once it starts I will not see him again until after the race when he is already showered and looking spiffy cheering me, my wife and whoever else we may have accumulated over the finish line.

I mention Shane because although we may not actually run together, I still consider him part of the team. I want to be clear that I am not fostering an us-versus-them/solo-versus-team runners mentality. I just want to make sure that you've asked yourself what it is exactly you want out of the event. If you're running with a team, make sure they know what you're there for. I've witnessed more than a few smiling, happy couples start a race looking like a recruitment poster for l-o-v-e only to end it with slightly different facial expressions. My guess, they didn't have the talk.

Know what you want out of the event and, if you team yourself with others, know what they expect as well. Be clear with them what you're in it for. If you play it this way then the only surprises on the course will be what the organizers/designers intended to surprise you with.

For our MMA/CQB brethren

For those who may not be aware, my publisher, Doug Werner, and I have authored more than a few books on MMA, boxing, submission wrestling, self-defense and conditioning as it specifically pertains to these areas. I know this book might seem a bit of a left turn or perhaps an odd change of course, but I'd like to offer a few words as to why this seemingly random title actually dovetails perfectly with the long-running theme of our work.

First, I love obstacle course events. They are quite simply a blast. If you have zero interest in MMA or self-defense, then allow that explanation to suffice and skip the upcoming rambling.

If you are a coach of real-world self-defense or have any interest in personal self-defense, then I heartily encourage you to read the next section because I'm talking directly to you.

Fight or flight

We've all heard of the titled dichotomy fight or flight. This dual choice, three word phrase is one that is, rightfully, on the tip of every street combatives/reality training enthusiasts' tongue. We all spout it when discussing questions of what's the best way to survive this or that scenario. We are able to delve into our memories of basic biology from high school and access our basic knee-jerk response to offer the usual "The fight or flight response is a reaction of the sympathetic nervous system and in times of stress ..." and so on and so forth.

We remind ourselves and others just how integral it is to choose flight whenever and wherever possible over the fight half of the dictum and to fight only if one must and then only until you are able to flee. Of course, this conversation is only for the street combatives folks among us. MMA and other sport brethren don't flee. As a matter of fact, sport combatives are merely scheduled beatings. If we had people fleeing left and right, there would be no sport and who would pay to see that?

... saying "I'm taking Krav Maga" sounds way cooler than "I'm taking urban sprint lessons."

There's certainly nothing wrong with providing behind the scenes biological processes that fuel the fight or flight dictum, and there's certainly nothing wrong with advising victims to flee (as a matter of fact, I think the moral thing to do is to advise a victim to flee whenever it is possible). What I do want to address is how much weight we give to one side of the fight or flight dictum compared with the scantiest of lip service we provide to the other. You with me yet?

If not, here's what I mean. We advise those who want honest advice on how to survive what may be the starkest and darkest time of their lives, and we tell them that if it is at all possible they should flee. And if it's not possible to flee, we then unload this or that eight-week course or such and such go-to moves to get them out of harm's way. (This discussion is not a criticism of any tactic or strategy. That is, it's not about what we teach, it's about what we don't teach). We spend all or (to give the benefit of the doubt) most of our time teaching or training ourselves and/or others how to fight. I get it, that's where the meat of the material is — the fun stuff. But are we assuming too much or providing a mixed message when we say "Flee at all costs" and then spend zero time working on fleeing and 100 percent of the time fighting?

> If there is a threat of any sort, it does you no good to remain near the threat. There are people whose job it is to get close to threats. If it is not your job — flee.

I think this might be due to a couple of reasons. First, like I said, this if where the fun stuff is. At a surface level saying "I'm taking Krav Maga" sounds way cooler than "I'm taking urban sprint lessons." Another factor may be the assumption that everyone knows how to run. Maybe. Consider the following.

If one reviews incidences of violence in mass/crowded situations, that is, areas where we finds lots of law-abiding people present when the violence begins, there is usually an initial freeze moment as good people try to assess a situation that is so far outside the ken of normal existence they are evaluating first, "Is this an actual threat?" and then wondering "What do I do?" (This is the fight or flight dilemma at its stripped down, most utilitarian level).

After the initial diagnosis that determines an actual threat, one of two things happens. Someone in the crowd or herd (I use the word "herd" with sincerity and respect as the herding instinct can be quite useful) will run, sparking others to do the same (the first to run, to get the herd moving is always a hero in my book). These people flee for any exit they can find, even in cases where the exact location of the threat is not determined (still a good call). Fleeing is a good thing — always. If there is a threat of any sort, it does you no good to remain near the threat. There are people whose job it is to get close to threats. If it is not your job — flee.

The second reaction is an unfortunate variation of a single theme — staying stock-still, literally frozen with shock at what is occurring and unable to shift the gear from neutral into either fight or flight (again, not a value judgment, just an observation — law-abiding people should never have to make the fight or flight decision, but, alas, it happens). A variation of the stock-still/frozen tactic is to run a brief distance and hide. Not good in almost every case. Those who are privy to what happened in Columbine are aware of the fates of some of those who hid. I could name instance after instance where hiding led to horrific consequences simply by dint of choosing to remain at the crime scene.

Our lessons from the instances of violence among crowds can be taken to the individual level as well.

Fleeing is a vitally useful tactic, and we are all correct in advising it as your go-to. But if we never train it, will it emerge when it is needed? We continually advise "Train it and it will come" and "Use it or lose it" in reference to combat skills. Yet how many of us work on any aspect of flight?

Let's not assume that doing a little roadwork each week and running a 5K or two each season means you are ready to flee. Fleeing at its base level will be a sprint. With that in mind, adding the occasional sprint session to any and all street combatives programs seems like a wise idea. In addition to this, I suggest adding the occasional sprint session in footwear and clothing that you actually wear on a day-to-day basis. If you wear footwear not conducive to sprinting, I suggest drilling kicking them off and hitting some sprints barefoot or in stocking feet.

Sprint variations may include multidirectional sprints where you move from cover to cover. Also, try adding crouch sprints where you keep a low profile as you run.

In addition to sprinting, it might be advisable to work on other, more unusual forms of locomotion. These might include rapid bear crawling to utilize cover, rapid hand and knee movement, and perhaps developing an elbow crawl/drag for very low cover.

It would also be wise to add mounting and navigating an obstacle or two to develop skill at getting yourself out of a variety of environments. I'm not suggesting that you need parkour ability, but it would be nice to

Side rant

Why do public/government schools utilize a policy of lockdown in the case of an intruder? That is, locking children into a classroom and instructing them to hide? When there is a fire or any other internal threat we train them them to flee the threat — a sound policy. I ask you, why in a situation where the threat is determined to be internal (as would be a fire or an intruder) we would advise keeping children (and adults for that matter) near the threat?

This is not a swipe at any teacher who has utilized this strategy. The teachers who did and do so are simply doing their best to follow a policy handed to them by people they assume had looked into it and were passing along their best judgment. Again, I would call attention to Columbine and ask why a lockdown and/or hide policy ever got off the ground. To be frank, it smacks of willfully ignorant criminal negligence.

End of rant.

know that you could sprint and hoist yourself up and out a 6-foot window if need be. Or climb up or down to a different level using rudimentary handholds and footholds.

We will be addressing several drills to assist in flight training in this book, and I urge you to consider adding them to your self-protection regimen. The main point of this discussion, though, is — when you utter the phrase "fight or flight" are you providing only lip service to half the equation?

For those who want more info regarding our take on self-protection, see our book *No Second Chance: A Reality-Based Guide to Self-Defense*.

HOO-AHH!!

Usually one's first look at an obstacle course event calls to mind the military, and there's a perfectly good reason for that. Most branches of the military worldwide use some form of obstacle course in basic training and often more intense obstacles for the elite special operations units.

A brief rundown of civilian obstacles reveal the mirror image of military utilitarianism:

Rope climbs
Barbed wire
Low crawls
Mud pits
Pugil sticks
Firehoses
Zip lines
Cargo nets
Horizontal ladders
Burma bridges
Horizontal and incline rope travels

These similarities are, of course, not accidental since from the very beginning big-kid-fun obstacle courses have been based on military precursors. As a matter of fact, this borrowing of devices or methods used to build warriors is not necessarily new. There is another sport out there, an Olympic one at that, that is based on military training.

Can you name the sport? I'll give you a hint — think leotards.

Yep, it's gymnastics. At its heart, much of its apparatus is a gussied up form of war training obstacles.

Horizontal ladders and high bars were originally used to train medieval warriors to scale castle walls.

Balance beams were used to train medieval soldiers to cross moats and other obstructions.

Pommel horses and vaulting horses — do you hear the root of the skill in the name? Knights and other mounted cavalry used similar devices to practice mounting and horseback mobility under full load (armor).

So you see taking devices and concepts with their origins in war and turning them into playthings is nothing new.

War and parkour

Staying with our military theme, you remember the fad a while back where every third commercial featured extremely agile athletes in urban environments making death defying leaps off rooftops, somersaults off parking garages, sprints up and over walls? You remember that breathtaking opening of the James Bond film *Casino Royale*? Cool stuff, huh?

Well, what these talented folks were doing was (and is) called freerunning, which, like gymnastics, is based on a military protocol. Let's work backward from cool Bond film opening to military application.

Freerunning is the more ornamental and acrobatic version of parkour.

Parkour is a civilian adaptation of military course obstacle technique transferred to the urban environment.

This military method was devised by George Hebert who was striving to build better French soldiers not merely via the conditioning effect built from the use of the obstacle course itself, but also by instructing soldiers in more efficient ways to navigate the course. He called this navigation instruction *parcours du combatant*, or roughly combat course.

I bring up this further war correlation not because we should all strive to be awesome freerunners or parkour traceurs (although that would be pretty awesome), but rather so we are aware that military minds have put some serious thought into the best way to navigate certain obstacles and terrains. And since these efficient minds have already pondered apparatus that were essentially theirs before we adopted them for fun, we would be remiss if we didn't adopt some of their knowledge along with their gear.

We won't be nearly as acrobatically dynamic as our talented freerunning and traceur brothers, but, then again, we have no need for that. We are not working in an urban environment or auditioning for a commercial. We are simply muddy folks with waterlogged shoes looking for the most efficient way to get from here to there. With that goal in mind, we will be closer to the military version of locomotion than the gravity defying Crouching Tiger crowd.

In the how-to and how not-to portion of this book you will encounter a mix of tips and techniques culled from Mr. Hebert, various military manuals from around the world, personal experience and other tips gathered along the way from fellow competitors.

Technique, Tactics & Strategies

We've talked attitude, origins, soldiers and civilians. Now it's time to get down to the nitty-gritty about what you need to know when you're getting down and dirty. This next section of the book is about technique and tactics and a little bit about strategy to allow you to better navigate the most likely obstacles and terrain you will encounter.

> *... while we will be providing specific advice in many instances, the wild card nature of these events means that adaptation and improvisation is in order.*

Keep in mind that while we will be providing specific advice in many instances, the wild card nature of these events means that adaptation and improvisation is in order. Use whatever suspiciously specific advice we offer as the template in your training sessions, but adapt, improvise and innovate when you hit the course. Maybe this or that bit of advice is not quite applicable in your unique situation. Use the advice in this book as a baseline, not as rock solid gospel truth.

Improvisation: Case in point
We were running an event situated in the foothills of the Appalachians, only in this case the term foothills did not do justice to the terrain. The topography was nothing like the beautifully worn trails one finds inside The Great Smoky Mountains National Park. These hills were acute angle inclines and declines covered with

scree (scree is loose rock/gravel ideal for turning ankles and initiating godawful falls).

We fell into stride with a couple of experienced trail runners who were kind enough to offer the advice of taking these treacherous downhill passages with either an exaggerated lean-back to keep your hips in front of you for speed control, or to use a galloping side-shuffle (we'll hit these in detail later). This advice worked well for many of the downhill switchbacks, but then the acute angle that we thought was mighty damned acute got even acuter (let's pretend that's a word).

In addition to the steep inclination, the switchbacks become shorter and sharper — the very definition of hair-pin turns — while the trail itself grew narrower. The downhill side of the trail was one unkind treacherous drop, and if you hit any uncontrolled overspeed at all via the lean-back, side-shuffle, or any other upright method, there was a high probability of overshooting the switchback and taking a plummet. Add scree and muddy shoes and our original desire to make good time on the downhill turned into a wish to just get down intact.

Everyone, experienced trail runners included, shifted to either a controlled plodding walk, or in some cases, a crab walk. The latter an exhausting but understandable option since this was steep, unstable stuff. To this point good technique (the lean-back and side-shuffle) helped us make good time. The improvised shift to walking or crab scuttling was wise, but much slower ...

Innovation time.

A band of us were walking or scuttling this treacherous downhill section when we heard behind us "Runner right!" This is the courtesy call to let you know that you've got runners coming up on your right who would like to pass. Only these guys weren't running. They were essentially riding a luge on one foot using

the loose scree as the lubricant instead of ice.

Eureka!

They were squatting, putting one foot in front and one foot directly underneath the hips — both feet were in contact with the ground.

The rear palm (the hand on the same side as the squatting leg) was loosely trailing on the ground behind them and functioning as a sort of balancing tool. They would rock forward on their hips and tuck the lead leg a bit to speed up, and lean back toward the rear hand to slow down. They were able to come out of this crouch directly to a stand to hit an upright stride when the terrain allowed it.

We watched these "runners" pass and then, without a word and almost in unison, we all adopted the innovation we had just witnessed. It worked beautifully. I find squatting on your subdominant leg (left leg if you're right-handed and vice versa) allows for better maneuvering into and out of the squat back into and out of a stride.

I have used this innovation many times since, particularly on muddy slopes. As soon as I encounter one, I don't even slow down — I just hit the squat luge and go.

The above story illustrates exactly what I'm talking about. Learn proper technique, train with proper technique, then rough up your training by getting it outside of controlled situations and never be afraid to adapt.

> Chances are if you already include running in your training, you have fallen naturally into a stride that works best for y-o-u, and you didn't even need a lesson.

A word or thirty about training
To make sure we're clear — this is the how-to section, as in how to do this or that maneuver. For those looking for info on how to incorporate these tactics and strategies into your training, you'll find that in the training menu portion of the book. There we'll give you specific training templates designed to develop these skills while building the peculiar strength and stamina specific to obstacle course events.

Take this info in stride
These events all have one thing in common — running. So if you're going to run, you're probably thinking I might as well be as efficient and awesomely up to date and trendy as I can be.

With that goal in mind, if you're gonna run efficiently, which style of stride do you choose? The Pose Method? Chi running, perhaps? How about running like a

Tarahumara Indian? Or a Kenyan for that matter? Or, why not a Jamaican? Seems to work for Usain Bolt. Oh, there's always the Romanov Method. (Yeah, the Pose Method and the Romanov Method are the same thing, I know. But I've seen instruction in these "same methods" that differed wildly on some points depending on who is doing the teaching. Maybe we can chalk these differences up to the adaptation/innovation thing we mentioned earlier).

Allow me to make this decision a little easier for you. Which method or stride will be the absolute best fit for you? (Drum roll, please!) Why, it's the one you already have. Chances are if you already include running in your training, you have fallen naturally into a stride that works best for y-o-u, and you didn't even need a lesson.

I know we all seek to be a bit better at what we do, that's only natural. Who doesn't want to be awesome, right? I am not denying the loads of anecdotal reports from any method you want to name of this or that dramatic improvement, but I would like to call your attention to the fact that good research into the efficacy of changing an athlete's stride revealed little to zero improvement over the long term and perhaps only incremental results over the short term. (You'll find sources at the end of this chapter.)

According to the smart guys in lab coats, running is such a natural bit of locomotion hardwired into our brains that tinkering with it may actually interfere in the long term as the athlete puts attentional/intentional energy (a glucose dump) into overriding what is a lifetime habit. It can be likened to switching your writing hand from your dominant hand to your subdominant simply because some blog or convincing article in *Penmanship World* struck a chord.

Of course, the argument can be made that all training in any physical endeavor is a hardwire overdrive, so let's just ignore these lab-coated meddlers. But consider this: Tasks that show measurable and lasting improvement under strict conditions is the training of skills that aren't necessarily natural, intuitive or encountered readily. A few tips on climbing a rope are often welcomed or needed because we don't often confront shimmying up a 20-foot length of 2-inch nautical rope in our day-to-day lives; whereas painstaking advice on how to specifically place one foot in front of the other and then doing it again seems to interfere with your cognitive processes.

This bit of interference is called choking.

There are many studies that show the best way to make skilled athletes choke is to have them become hyperaware of just how they perform some given task they have trained so much that it has become second nature. If we can bollix up pros by making them overthink what they do, it follows that we can easily bollix up ourselves by second guessing what we already do naturally. (Again, all the science-y sources at the end of this section).

Before you completely discount what my sources and I say, consider the following. Stride training is often relegated to ideal conditions on tracks, roads and clean trails. Now compare the ideal stride environment with the muddy, scree covered route that you will travel in water logged, mud-laden shoes. Will these variables affect that perfect form you've been working on? Oh, you know it will.

What will you do when you encounter these variables? Run the adaptation calculus so that you can best adapt the perfect stride to the less than perfect conditions? Sure, that's doable. You can also keep on running and trust the fact that evolution has designed humans for bipedal loco-motion and has millennia of evolu-tionary adjustments behind the wisdom of how we travel on two feet. You will, in all likelihood, navigate these varying terrains and conditions just fine without any need for cognitive thought.

High Intensity Training (HIT) has been shown time and time again to reap signifi-cant rewards for those who use it as the fundamental basis for physical training.

Still not convinced? Let's look at stride training in the context of cost-to-benefit analysis. Compare the time (and perhaps money) that it requires to run this or that drill to build the new stride in hopes that you will maintain that perfection so few athletes actually do who complete stride training. (Again, I'm relying on the data here, this ain't me with a stride bone to pick). Add in the time and cognitive effort required to completely override how you naturally run. Compare the time invested in this endeavor with the time that could have been invested in what has been shown in study after study to actually work — High Intensity Training.

HIT

High Intensity Training (HIT) has been shown time and time again to reap significant rewards for those who use it as the fundamental basis for physical training. (As a matter of fact this manual will use the HIT method to build your obstacle course conditioning while building specific nonintuitive skills.) If we are attracted to perfect stride training because we have a Jones for efficiency, then we should be all the more attracted

... where should we spend our limited training hours — working a method with questionable results or working one with verified results?

to HIT training because it is not only efficient, but quantifiably and qualifiedly proven to be efficient.

Furthermore, if we are serious about efficiency, we would then compare the time costs between a method of training that may not manifest once the blush falls off the rose of our initial training honeymoon period (stride work) and how much HIT training we could have been doing with that time. In other words, even if we are charitable about the efficiency of stride training, we have to ask where should we spend our limited training hours — working a method with questionable results or working one with verified results?

If you are a devotee of this or that stride method and you just know in your heart of hearts that you have benefited enormously from your stride relearning program, then by all means ignore all the data and arguments I have offered and run how you see fit. But how exactly do you disentangle what gave you your measured benefit? How can you tell where your stride is responsible for your speed or endurance and where it might be the actual endurance/speed training you have put in. I'm just saying.

In a nutshell, you will need to run to condition for these events. But less important than how you run is the fact that you do run and that you run with intensity. And that your running must include the sort of random variables that most closely duplicate the odd nature of obstacle course work. More on this in the next section, but first those promised sources.

Sources and suggested reading
Which Comes First, Cardio or Weights? Fitness Myths, Training Truths and Other Surprising Studies from the Science of Exercise by Alex Hutchinson. A mighty fine book that includes the stride study info.

The First 20 Minutes: Surprising Science Reveals How We Can Exercise Better, Train Smarter, Live Longer by Gretchen Reynolds. A good basic overview of what we actually know about exercise and what we don't know.

Wrong: Why Experts Keep Failing — And How to Know When Not to Trust Them by David H. Freedman. While not a book specifically about training, it is my favorite of the bunch because it opens our eyes as to just how much of what we consume and presume to be pertinent info may be based in zip. Most useful.

Paleofantasy: What Evolution Really Tells Us About Sex, Diet, and How We Live by Marlene Zuk. A well-done debunk of some current trendy notions—barefooters beware.

HOW TO RUN

Isn't that title hypocritical? I spend a few pages telling you not to listen to anyone tell you how to run, and here I go doing just that. Not really. I am not advising you how to run in the "put this foot right here and exactly like this" manner. My concerns are what attitude to run with and what conditions to run in. The advice regarding attitude can be summed up via a maxim used by elite special forces:

Let your training reflect battlefield conditions.

If we assume our mudslicked, outdoor obstacle course is our big kids' battlefield, then how much sense does it make to run on a flat track or road or (God forbid) a treadmill? It is advisable to pass on these less than battlefield reflective running environments and opt for running outside whenever possible. And when outdoors, strive for off-road trail work — the hillier and more varied the terrain the better.

If you live in an area without trails, you're not out of luck. You still have an outside at the very least, so take your runs outside. And in your outside/non-trail environment look for routes that provide hills and sloping/slanting terrains. Perhaps cut through parking lots and pass over a curb or two, hop a bike rack here and there. If there's a puddle, run through it with a 4-year-old's abandon.

Again, we are simply talking attitude and conditions. In the menu section, you will find specific workout templates for several running options. Remember that all are meant to be performed with the described attitude and environment variability.

Hills can be hell

Hill running, uphill or downhill, can take a toll on your legs and stamina. It's worth taking a couple of moments to pass along a few ideas that may lighten the load.

UPHILL TACTICS & STRATEGY

Posture

As a rule, all your running will be a bit more effi- cient if you maintain an upright posture. Pitching forward at the waist or rounding the shoulders forward can lead to increased load on the quadriceps. While this load is not necessarily detrimental in flat work, a tendency to lean forward or round the shoul- ders will become more acute as you run uphill. This is where that increased load on the quads will take its toll.

Don't reach

There is often a temptation to treat steep uphill pas- sages like a flight of stairs, more so if the terrain is stony and actually resembles stair steps. But it is recom- mended that you step on every stair rather than hustle up two at a time.

This overreaching requires more muscle mass to climb and eats a good bit of energy. You don't necessarily know how many "stairs" you will be climbing that day, so backing off on bounding may be a wiser plan of action.

Overstep

Don't think that because I suggest you kibosh bounding "upstairs" with vigor that I am encouraging you to take it slow. There is an alternative to over-reaching and that is to overstep.

Overstepping is simply taking three steps when two steps will do. When you hit an incline, don't reach forward with your strides because this will turn your run into a climb. Instead, focus on reducing reach thus allowing you to maintain good posture as much as possible and therefore conserving energy. For a mental picture, you will be taking short choppy steps up the hill

as opposed to big muscular bounds. Nibble at the hill, don't take big bites.

Four-wheeling

When the terrain is right on the cusp of too steep to run upright and not quite steep enough to turn into an actual climb, you can opt to four-wheel it.

To four-wheel is essentially hitting a bear crawl variant on a slanted terrain. Your hands will touch lightly on the ground where they will assist by pulling you along. Most of your power (a good 90 percent) will still be driven from the legs.

If you keep your hips shifted above your feet relative to your angle of inclination to the hill, you will lighten the load on your arms and legs and travel more efficiently than if you shift your hips further forward or rearward.

DOWNHILL TACTICS & STRATEGY

Overspeed

If (if) you can see your downhill terrain clearly and have judged there to be no issues with hitting over-speed, than do so to gain time and conserve energy.

To overspeed downhill you will take a slight lean of the entire body forward (not simply at the waist) that will propel you to move forward down the hill. Your stride will naturally fall into place to keep you from pitching forward, but ...

Don't reach

I repeat the advice from the uphill section.
Overreaching on the downhill feels mighty natural, but just as with the uphill, it can begin to take its toll on the legs from absorbing the downhill impact. A down-hill overreach is essentially a series of leaps with mul-tiple G-force and one-legged landings. A tough course full of such repeated shock absorptions will play havoc with your legs as the race goes on.

Overstep

The uphill advice holds here as well. If you use the for-ward lean to assist your overspeed and kill your temp-tation to reach by "taking three steps when two will do," you will have both the benefit of the downhill to assist your speed and the chopping rhythm of your stride to keep the shock impact on your legs to a minimum.

Lean back

When the way is a bit steeper than you'd like, you're unsure of the footing or you've got switchbacks to navigate, you may want to reverse the overspeed posture and lean a bit backward at the waist. The backward lean allows you to get a better handle on your speed.

Side-shuffle

On a downhill where straight down travel feels too fast, or if you need to provide a bit of R & R for taxed legs while staying on the move, the side-shuffle can be of help.

Face your dominant side in a half turn toward the downhill (if you're a rightie, your side shoulder and hip will be advanced toward the bottom of the hill).

You will essentially be taking short skipping hops down the hill while maintaining your quasi-sideways position. Feel free to switch the side facing downhill, but we find that most prefer their dominant side to the fore.

Four-wheeling
Just as in the uphill, we may have a hill that is somewhere between upright striding and an out-and-out climb down where your chest must face the climbing surface.

To four-wheel downhill, drop back onto your hands in a crab-walk position. Shift your hips toward your feet in relation to the incline of the hill — shifting the hips to this position takes unwelcome excess load off the arms and hands. Take short steps with the hands and feet.

Squat luge
We've already discussed this useful technique. It is a good way to negotiate slippery and steep downhills.

Comfort for those who sweat the running

Some out there may be mighty attracted to the prospect of obstacle course races, but simply do not like to run. I've met and conversed with quite a few who feel this way and, I'll admit, I sympathize with that camp. I lean toward this inclination myself. You might be wondering, "I hate running, and I simply don't want to make myself miserable adding more running to my training. Can I still do one of these events? Will I be miserable?"

There are more obstacle-loving, running-adverse types out there than you might realize.

My advice is, if you're interested in these events (why else would you be reading this book) and you are a less than enthusiastic fan of running, you should still get out there and play. Enjoy the obstacles, the camaraderie, but consider this.

Do some running in your training, but don't overdo it. If running is not your thing, then it makes no sense to do more of something you dislike simply so you can go do something that you think you would like to do. Get the most bang for your running buck using our running templates and possibly consider using the walk-up/run-down strategy.

This is exactly what it sounds like. Choose a comfortable jogging pace on the flats, pick up that speed on the downhills, and each time you are faced with an uphill — walk it. No harm in that. Don't think less of yourself if you choose this strategy. You will see plenty of fit-looking folks doing just what I described. There are more obstacle-loving, running-adverse types out there than you might realize.

The main thing to remember at these events is to have fun. If it's about the competitive time, go ahead and run. But remember those earlier caveats regarding the verity of running times.

You're the boss — run how you want and when you want.

Did I mention the mud?
These things, as rule, are great big muddy affairs and you're going to get plenty muddy — in your shoes, face, hair and mouth. During clean-up, you will find yourself the proud owner of mud-caked private nooks and crannies, areas you thought would be protected by boxers and panties. (Advice on cleaning your naughty nooks and dirty crannies in the logistics section.)

Since there will be mud, a few words as to how to run on and through mud will be useful. Any time you have to submerge a foot into mud, you are dealing with the possibility of losing a shoe. To reduce that possibility, consider using the tip-toe method.

Tip-toe
Approach each mud pit, swamp or bog, whether it be ankle deep or chest high, like a ballerina. Reduce your stride and switch to running on your tip-toes, that is, stay on the balls of your feet as you navigate these sections.

More often than not, it is the heel-down portion of the stride that allows the shoe to be sucked off the foot. Maintaining a tip-toe approach reduces the suction. It's not fool proof, but it's a 90 percenter on effectiveness and that's pretty good odds.

If you approach a mud flat, that is, a flat or semi-inclined mudslicked terrain that is not boggy enough to sink into, but slick enough to drop you on your butt, you will want to adopt the snowshoe stride.

Snowshoe

To snowshoe, reduce your stride to keep your feet underneath your hips. Here you will not tip-toe but aim to place the entire sole of the foot (flat of the shoe) on the ground with each short step. The increased surface area will help you stay on your feet. Remember to keep full sole contact and resist the natural tendency to return to your usual heel-toe walking motion.

Side note

We hit an event in northern Kentucky called the Mudathlon. It was a 5K course with obstacles on the lean side and yet the entire course was so uniformly mudslicked, it became one of the more challenging and fun experiences of that season.

There were 25-yard sections where I took approximately five falls per traverse. Watching those around me confirmed that apparently we humans don't do well under these conditions. Snowshoeing didn't eliminate falls, but it did lead to fewer than average.

Shoes, almost shoes, no shoes and shoe laces

Let's talk gear for a moment. This conversation might best be served in the logistics section where we will

discuss other wardrobe tips, but since we need to train in what we will run in, let's discuss it now.

What sort of shoes should I wear? I'm going to refrain from giving you specific brand endorse-ments as I see a good variety of shoes delivering good traction/results. There are now shoes purportedly designed specifically for such events, and there's no harm in trying these out to see if they fit your needs and pocket book. As a rule, you will find any shoe that has good off-road tread (trail-running shoes might actu-ally be the ideal) and that drains well to be an excellent choice.

Draining is essential. A good obstacle course shoe might not be the best everyday shoe as it allows water to easily enter the shoe vault and soak the foot and sock. Not ideal for that inadvertently stepped-in puddle in the parking lot, but oh so useful on a wet, muddy course.

These porous shoes will be your best friend on the course. Yes, water and mud will enter easily, but they also allow for faster, more efficient drain. Mudcaked soles on your shoes can add additional weight and energy burn, there's no sense in adding to that energy deficit by sloshing around in poor draining, water-

> *The soldiers who make up the Go-Ruck Challenge cadre have a term for these minimal-sole gloved shoes: Five-finger death punch.*

logged shoes. A word or two about what you might want to avoid.

You know those curious-looking shoes with the individual toe compartments that fit your feet like a glove? Yeah, I've owned a few pair of them myself. I'm not going to name names since I've got something a little less than complimentary to pass along.

Despite the hype and how well they seemingly perform in a predictable environment, they may not be your ideal obstacle course choice. Why?

First, recall those books I recommended in the stride section? Have a look-see at the actual nonpartisan objective studies that offer the actual benefits of bare-foot or semi-barefoot running. Despite the hype, it may not be all it's cut out to be. And to all of the barefoot/minimal shoe enthusiasts out there, before you get your feathers all ruffled, have a look at the science and then hit the course with them. Make up your own mind. I'm only a messenger here.

Second, these shoes, as mentioned, feature individual toe compartments as a design feature. Now what I'm about to say is simply anecdotal evidence of what happened to me, which can lead one to believe that either the shoes may have issues or I'm an exceptionally clumsy human being (we can't rule that out).

While training for an event, I moved off trail to run upstream through a shallow creek bed that was strewn with small, medium and large river rocks. A misplaced step allowed a small rock between the left little toe and the remainder of the foot. As I came out of that step I felt a sharp pain. I stopped, looked down and saw that my little toe was pointing at a right angle to the rest of my foot. Having owned this toe for 46 years, that seemed a little out of character.

I sat down on the creek bank and carefully peeled this tight, wet, glove-like shoe off my foot and broken toe and reset it. I am more than a few miles from where I need to be and have to wedge this thing back onto my foot — fun stuff. I do so, and after some compensations to my stride, I return to running (albeit at a much reduced tempo as I am babying the injury). Wanna guess what happens next?

Same thing. This time the right foot.

These glove-like shoes also sport minimal sole as a design feature. This minimal sole can work against you on two other counts (besides clumsy creek bed running). Running on scree or any pebbled or jagged rock surface with these gloved shoes is very difficult. If you do enough of these events, you will hit these surfaces in more than a few course segments. These jagged surfaces coupled with these minimal soles can turn your run into a Tony Robbins motivational firewalk gone horribly wrong.

The second minimal sole problem is they're bad for load bearing. A great many of these events will require you to pick up something heavy and lug it about. In my experience I've lugged sandbags, logs, rocks, big bits of concrete, buckets of water, truck tires and sections of telephone pole. You may be required to lug these things up and down hills and over and under some less than serene terrain. The minimal sole under load increases the sensitivity to every bit of uncomfy terrain and plays hell with the foot in general due to lack of any true arch support.

There is a mighty interesting (and rewarding) event called The *Go-Ruck Challenge* where you get to stay with a 30-person team over multiple hours getting a tiny taste of what it might be like to be in special forces training. Your 30-person crew is led through the challenge by actual special forces personnel.

A feature of this multihour event is lots and lots and lots of moving under load. The soldiers who make up the *Go-Ruck Challenge* cadre have a term for these minimal-sole gloved shoes: Five-finger death punch. I've been told by these men truly in the know that they've never had a participant who has shown up wearing these finish the event.

Hey, all you barefoot runners out there, I'm not trying to rain on your Christopher McDougall, *Born to Run* parade, just want to point out that if there are concerns with the minimal shoes on these courses, extrapolate these potential problems to no shoes at all.

More anecdotal info. Any time I have come across an

athlete in the middle of a race who was making a go of it barefoot I always say, "Man, toughing it out barefoot, good on you. How's that working out?" The answer I have invariably received thus far is, "Big mistake. Don't do it."

Expensive shoes? Would you like to keep them?

Again, this conversation might best be served in the logistics section, but we've had so much to say about shoes in the past few pages that it seems a little illog-

ical if we didn't say a word or two about how to keep those shoes we've talked about so much. Many of the shoes we've discussed that work best for these events (and even those that are less than ideal) cost more than a couple of tanks of gas and that's saying something these days. If you have your eye on more than one race, we can surmise that if you lose or toss your shoes at each event we are looking at eating into your retirement.

My wife and I have run (thus far) every single event in the same pair of shoes. Never had one come off, and that's saying something, because losing a shoe in mud pits, bogs or silt sinks is mighty common. I attribute our astounding shoe-keeping powers to three things …

Luck. I would not be surprised that if after keying in that last paragraph that I went out and lost both shoes in my very next event. We can never rule out luck, good or bad.

Double-knotting. It's exactly what it sounds like, once you tie your standard bow-knot we all learned as children, grasp the loops and repeat the process one more time. Pull both of your knots tight, tight, tight.

Tying your shoes on the transverse. Wha? Believe it or not, you can predict, more often than not, who will lose their shoes. You can tell which shoes are susceptible to coming untied simply by looking at their knots. This little prediction test works whether someone is in a race or simply walking in the mall.

Take a gander at their shoes and see which way the 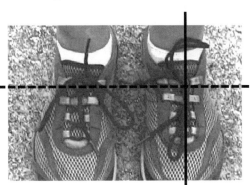 ends of the bow are facing. Facing toward the toe and ankle? This has a greater chance of coming untied. Ends of the bow facing toward the inside and outside of the foot (transverse position) give increased odds of keeping that shoe knotted.

If you check out your own knot tying, and you naturally tie on the transverse, you're good to go. If not, reorient to the transverse on the initial knot and the double-knot, pull both of these tightly and welcome yourself to snug shoe territory.

If for some reason you do not naturally tie on the transverse and your brain simply can't wrap itself around
how to reorient (it happens), have a look at the *TED
Talk* by Terry Moore and he'll walk you through it in
under three minutes.

http://www.ted.com/
talks/terry_moore_how_to_tie_your_shoes.html

What about duct tape?

How about wrapping shoes in duct tape to keep them
on?

That's an excellent question. You'll see shoes with a
few loops of tape wrapped around the arch of the foot
and over the laces. People also double up that arch
looping with a loop or two passed around the ankle.
You'll see a few folks who go the whole hog and wrap
the entire shoe in duct tape until it resembles some
low-quality Apollo astronaut boot.

Here are two things to consider if you are pondering
duct tape.

We've gone out and purchased ourselves some expensive footwear to get the job done on a slick, wet and
muddy course. As we already know, part of getting the
job done is good traction from the trail-running tread
and good drainage from the foot vault.

Increased load. With water weight in mind, are we
now really going to reduce our expensive drainage
system by blocking up the drain mesh with tape?

Traction deficit. Do we actually think applying slick silver-backed duct tape to the bottom of our shoes, which reduces our tread surface area and then adding water and mud to the already slick tape surface is the best way to maximize traction?

This traction deficit may not seem like much on the ground (and that's a maybe), but consider how you'd feel about running across mud-covered 2-inch wide beams to cross a gully with a significant drop with that reduced traction before you tape up with abandon.

Side note
I gave the taping a shot in one event to see if it was a better way to go than simply double-knotting and transverse tying. It was then that I encountered the poor drainage and reduced traction I just mentioned.

I also found that during post or rope climbs or slides where a squat luge was needed that the tape unraveled due to the friction on various portions of the shoe. I had to stop and undo all my methodical taping work. I unraveled and attempted to tear wet, twisted duct tape, which is not the easiest tape to tear under the best of conditions. The unraveling process led to laces becoming entangled in the wet sticky mass, which led to untying, which led to having to retie the double-knot with the shoes laces already wet and saturated with mud. The muddy laces led to more untying and so on and so on.

LOOK BEFORE YOU LEAP

Before we discuss a few tips on how to leap, jump, hop and cavort with abandon, let's get the preflight safety lecture out of the way.

Just like the heading says, please look before you leap over that log, jump over that fence, drop off that high wall or take the plunge off a ridge into that muddy slurry of water below.

These events are fun but hold an element of risk. After all, you've got competitive humans leaping, crawling and dashing about left and right. With all that wild action, there is bound to be an injury or two.

Usually these injuries are of the blown ankle or tweaked knee variety. Many ankle sprains tend to be luck of the draw terrain twists — poor placement on uncertain surfaces, that sort of thing. But almost as often these injuries result from an understandably zealous desire to approach the course with unchecked attack.

I'm all for giving it all you got, but look before you leap on any landing where you can not directly see your landing surface. This includes drops off the other side of any wall, rope, net, boom or other under-and-over obstacle. As a rule — sight before flight.

Just because there is nice terra firma on the run-up to a wall does not guarantee that will be the case on the other side. I've encountered 4-foot walls that dropped to 10 feet; fence vaults that landed you into a tangle of tree roots waiting to trap and snap unsuspecting tibias; easy plunges into waist high slurried water that wound up containing submerged shin and femur busting cross ties and lurking cypress roots; walls that you had to hoist yourself over and the drop on the other side was to a muddy slope ready to tweak knees or supply groin tears to the unsuspecting.

If you can't spot your landing area and/or have any doubts about what's on the other side, what's down below, or what's in that water — then proceed with caution. Look before you leap.

STICK THAT LANDING

This is cart before the horse territory. Before we discuss being airborne, we will discuss how to return to earth. Like running, most leaps, jumps and vaults are intuitive skills. But what is rather counterintuitive is shock absorption upon descent.

If you stand your standard human on a 24-inch platform (not high at all in course terms) and ask them to jump off, a marked majority will land with a slight bend in the knees, usually no more than 45 degrees of bend, with a tendency to flex the quadriceps to brace the landing.

The result of these braced landings is a flat-footed jolt that may not feel like much of a problem. And it's not a problem if there are only a few in your course. But if there are only one or two 24-inch jumps in your course, you've signed up for one weak-ass event.

Our G-force laden problem begins to rear its ugly head when we have multiple braced landings in our future linked with the likelihood that some of these landings will be above and beyond our 24-inch example. With lots and lots of G-forces to overcome, it is wise to utilize educated shock absorption from the get-go.

Braced landing

Squat landing

The core of proper landing technique is to exaggerate all landings to kill the natural tendency to brace. To do this, simply endeavor to land in a

Squat landing

semi-squat to a deep squat for any drop 18 inches or higher. Never land in a braced, squat position. Allow your legs to fold beneath you upon landing until they have absorbed most of the G-force by "going with the landing" as opposed to bracing and "taking it."

Slap Landing
Another useful tool for landings 24 inches and higher is to reach for the ground with your hands. Not in an attempt to add two more limbs for a braced landing, but to enforce a deeper squat landing to help absorb G's from the higher drop. To remove the tendency to reach and brace with your arms, think of landing in a deep squat and slapping the ground with your palms rather than posting on the ground with your hands.

Roll Landings
For even higher drops, I propose the following technique to diffuse some of the increased G's imposed by the increased height. After your slap landing, immediately hit a shoulder roll that allows you to return to a squat at the end of the roll and then back into your stride.

● Think, slap landing.
● Pick a shoulder to roll over.
● Tuck your chin to your chest.
● Move both hands toward your centerline to resist the temptation to post during the roll.
● Roll at a diagonal from shoulder to opposite hip to reduce both spinal column and kidney contact with the ground.

The roll landing is one continuous movement from drop, to slap landing, to roll, to return stride.

Important —Take terrain into consideration. If you are dropping onto scree or any such surface with protruding rocks or any other iffy ground, do not use the shoulder roll. Yes, the diagonal path of your roll will reduce vital innards contact, but we're not all made of that adamantine wolverine skeleton stuff. Use your noggin' in regard as to when to roll.

GROUND CONTROL TO MAJOR TOM

Now that we know how to land, let's discuss getting into the air in the first place. Most all jumping, leaping, hopping and one and two-foot takeoffs that you encounter on the course will be intuitive calls depending on your particular terrain and athletic abilities. What is an easy two-footed jump for some may be an all-out run up and leap for another. And again, terrain will often dictate your approach.

Where I may be of some help is to advise you in planning your trajectory.

Often when there is a gap of any distance to be crossed, there is a common inclination to focus on the "how far" part of the gap. Yes, we do have to cover that distance, but not in a straight line. As a hard fast rule, the wider the gap, the higher you must jump. You must think up and across — not simply across. If you plan for the highest point in your trajectory to be at the middle of the gap to be crossed, you're on the right track.

This rule holds true even when the gap begins from a higher elevation. Do not simply jump down and over the gap, but up and across.

See next page.

Jumping from high to low
Jumping up and over with a slap landing to
finish

JUMP THE FUEL, NOT THE FIRE

Many of these events offer a dramatic pre-finish line ending in the form of a flame barrier to be leapt across. Fun stuff and a great photo op as nothing says unforgettable weekend like "I went through fire to do this!"

There are a few of us out there that sweat this little flame hop, so I want to put your minds at ease. Ain't nothing to it. I know you might eyeball the top of the flames and think to yourself, "There's no way I can jump that high."

The good news is that you don't have to jump that high. You need to jump the fuel, not the flame. More often than not, this flame barrier is a line of burning material no more than 12-15 inches high and that's the highest you need to jump.

Your brief time in the flame will cause you no pain, and you will not be burned. Think back to when you were a kid and played with a candle. Did you ever rapidly swipe your finger back and forth through the flame? You didn't get burnt, right? If you didn't do this as a kid and still sweat the flame jump, go grab a candle right now and set your mind at ease.

Same thing with the flame jump. Your time inside the flame is so inconsequential that I'd be surprised if you even felt the memory of heat.

Jump the fuel, not the fire and you'll be fine.

SHOCKING TRUTH

If jumping through flames is no biggie, how about electrical shocks? Some of these courses feature an electrical shock, but relax, it's not many.

Ready for the words of comfort? Well, I'm not gonna lie to you, getting shocked sucks. That's all there is to it. My only words of comfort are that it's not dangerous to be shocked by the voltages these courses are allowed to use. The voltages, while uncomfortable, are definitely tolerable.

Also, the shocks are of such brief duration that your pre-shock anxiety about how you'll endure any shock you might receive on the course lasts far longer and does more to limit you than simply taking the shock and getting on with it.

I now offer the following tips to improve your reaction to the shock.

Close your mouth. When the juice hits, you will clench your jaw, no sense in having a tongue or lip caught between your teeth adding to the discomfort.

Hit the Speed. There is an understandable tendency to slow down as you approach any electrical hazard in

67

anticipation of what's to come. But look at it this way — slowing down means you'll be shocked for even longer. Hit the speed and get it over with.

The shocks can come in three forms — water hazards, wire dangles and hot bars. Here's a few tips on how to navigate each of these.

Water hazard. Here you move through ankle to waist deep water as the juice hits you. Keep your mouth closed, your speed up as much as safety will allow, and keep your hands and arms out of the water. Touching your hands to the water adds another path for the current to have fun with.

Wire dangles. Here the shock is delivered via dangling wire leads that you must run through (not every wire will be hot, but it's no use to pick and choose).

Keep your mouth closed. Hit the speed. Don't dally by trying to pivot and spin trying to get out unshocked. Get it over with. Make fists and keep your arms tucked to your body. Pulling the arms tight allows you to reduce contact with the wire dangles and closing the fists prevents your hands from convulsively closing on and staying on a wire lead if you are hit with juice.

No

Hot bars. Here you have horizontal uprights to climb. These metal horizontal rungs may have the occasional jolt surging through them. In these cases use the thumbless grip on the bar. Going thumbless allows you to retract your hand when convulsed.

There you go, a few tips to make one of the more anxiety-provoking classes of obstacles a little less shocking than they actually are.

RUNNING THE GAUNTLET

Some events near the end of the race feature a couple of kind folks wielding pugil sticks. Think of a staff with padding on each end. Their job is to give you a hearty thump or two as you make the last stretch for the finish line.

This is another one of those, "Oh, man, is that gonna hurt?" obstacles. No, of course not. The thumps are delivered with measured kindness and are all in good fun, so no need getting worried or all testosteroned up anticipating some malicious beatdown and payback scenario.

There are two ways you will see the pugil sticks utilized. One is a hale and hearty whack or two on the

body or legs as you make the run-through. The head is off limits, or so I am told. The other is when the pugil stick is held horizontally used to block your passage rather than spank your butt.

In either case, I suggest lowering your base and shooting through full steam ahead. You see, with the head being off limits and the actual "damage" you will incur being nothing to sweat, I advise getting low and sprinting through as if you were going to tackle their hips (but don't do that). Getting low and driving reduces target area for the thumpers and gives you some leg drive versus the blockers.

WHY ARE YOU HERE?

Since we've just discussed a few classes of obstacles that are more about (forgive the expression) nutting up and getting it over with, I think a word or two about attitude is in order.

We're all attracted to these events because we're wondering how we'll do, how we will stack up when faced with this or that challenge. That's what this is all about, right? Well, fun is word number one and then comes that little nudge of curiosity that says, "Man, I hope I do all right." You will.

What I want to help with is making sure you perform up to your expectations and not get in your own way.

It's common to hear people sweating fire hazards, shock obstacles, obstacles with any significant height and cold water swims. We've all got our buttons. You'll hear folks in the queue waiting their turn to do this or that thing feeding their anxiety with remarks like "That flame sure looks high!" or "Does the shock hurt much?" or "Wow, that's sure going to be cold!"

My advice to you when you feel a little overanxious is to stifle the gripe and get on with it.

I get it — it's hard not to ponder what you're a little less than sure about. But I ask you, what did you sign up for? You're here to swim in that water, right? You're going to climb up that cargo net, go over the boom and climb down the other side, right? You're going to eat that shock and move on, right? What I'm saying is you signed up to push yourself a little, test yourself a bit and obstacles such as these aren't really a surprise. Heck, you're reading a book about them. It's not like you walked out of Starbucks and stumbled into a Tough Mudder.

My advice to you when you feel a little overanxious is to stifle the gripe and get on with it. Remember that you signed up to have fun, not talk yourself out of fun. Getting yourself all worked up about this or that course segment will not help you in any way and, to be honest, it's a little less than interesting or helpful conversation for your fellow teammates.

Don't be that guy. Don't be that gal. You're here to swim in cold water, climb up and down high things and other challenging tasks, so shut up and just do it — and smile when you're at it!

SHOWING YOU THE ROPES

Most of these events have a rope climb or two somewhere on the course, so a few pointers on shimmying our butts up and down ropes are appropriate. If you lack the upper body strength to climb, don't sweat it, the conditioning portion of this book will get you there. If you are iffy at climbing, the following tips should help.

First, the good news. I've not been in an event yet where the ropes to be climbed didn't sport a knot or three to lug our bad selves up and down the rope. For those of us who are used to climbing 15-20-foot lengths of unknotted rope, this is a gladsome sight.

And now for the bad news. Unless the rope you use to train on is water-logged and slicked with mud from all the prior climbers, you might be in for an impolite awakening.

Reach High. Most of the mud will be on the lower third of the rope because most folks never get past this portion of the climb. The entire length of the rope will most likely be mudslicked, but most of the gooey fun is at the bottom.

Stack your hands above a knot if you can. This isn't integral, but it can be a help.

Grip from the bottom up. When you clench the rope in your fist, start the pressure from your little finger (the pinky) and then run the pressure to the ring finger, middle finger, to index finger and finally the thumb as an overlay on top of two fingers (index and middle).

Most folks have a tendency to grip from the top down where the grip pressure is asserted by the thumb and index and middle finger lock. This grip underutilizes the ring and little fingers. Bottom up gripping increases your contact surface area with the unsure traction of the rope and equalizes the grip pressure staving off the lactic burn in your forearms a little longer.

This is a subtle point, but give it a shot. If you are already a good rope climber, try five back-to-back top-down grip rope climbs today and five back-to-back bottom-up climbs tomorrow and ask yourself if you can feel the difference.

Use blade-to-blade pressure. You are unlikely to climb arms alone, he-man style on a muddy rope, so you need to get your feet into the game.

Since in all likelihood you will be wearing shorts (or some variation

thereof to cut down on water weight — more on this later) you ain't gonna want to thread that rope between the tender meat of your lovely thighs or behind your calves. Open raw rope burns are no fun for anyone except those who pay dearly for the privilege in certain consenting adult establishments.

You want to pinch grip the rope between the blades of both feet (outside edges of the feet).

There are various other ways to lock-down a rope with your feet, but I am advocating the blade-to-blade pressure over others because it does not pass the rope over your laces. Mud as a lubricant plus the rope friction usually result in untied shoes, even those with transverse double knots.

Inchworm. Use the inchworm method to reduce the number of pulls on the rope you make to conserve energy.

● Reach as high as you can and hit your bottom-up grip.
● Tuck your legs as high as possible and hit blade-to-blade pressure.
● Reach as high as you can with one hand using a bottom-up grip.
● And then the other hand using a bottom-up grip.
● Repeat the inchworm steps.
● Continue to the top until you can slap the bell with one hand.

Don't slide down. Do I even need to say this? Makes for open wounds, people. Reverse your inchworm instead.

Don't drop or jump. That is, until you are certain of your landing. Remember, look before you leap.

Pull a Hobie. Talented Spartan uber-competitor Hobie Call uses a foot to ring the bell. If you trust your grip, do what works for one of the best.

Rope swing tactics

If you are fortunate enough to encounter a rope swing, this is how you can make sure you stick your rope approach and landing:

● Don't slow down as you approach the rope — keep your pace.
● Leap (not jump) into the rope — not upward. Jumping up in this case limits your travel trajectory possibly causing you to fall short of your landing zone.
● Sight the rope as you approach and grasp it with your hands — not reaching up —and pull your body upward and to the rope allowing your center of mass to give you travel inertia.

● Let go before you land. This is a tough one to follow as there is a huge tendency to want to reach toward the ground with your feet. Reaching with the legs while trying to keep that rope in your grip will cause you to lose your balance, fall short and fall on your butt. Let go before your landing and allow your initial dive at the rope to carry you across.

Horizontal / incline ropes

Occasionally you will have the good fortune to have to traverse straight across an obstacle via a horizontally hung rope (some-times the rope may have a slight upward inclination).

● Travel head first.
● Use hand-over-hand travel (see page 95).
● Use foot-over-foot travel. Hook with the backs of your heels (see page 97).

You should find the preceding the best way to go. You may occa-sionally see a few brave souls attempting to travel on top of the rope with a crotch shimmy. Not a bad technique if you are wearing military cammies, but more than likely you ain't.

Rope walls

Often there will be a rope dan-gling next to a vertical wall or cliff (I've got one memorable 50-foot cliff climb in mind — a blast!) or the rope may be there to assist you over a slanted wall (not as easy as it sounds if firehoses are hitting you). The technique for vertical or slanted walls is the same.

● Use hand-over-hand technique.

● Don't reach. Travel with short strokes approximately head-high pulling to chest level with each stroke.
● Use the entire sole of the foot to stay in contact with the wall. Balancing on the toes reduces friction and is exhausting on long hauls.

Take short steps and keep your feet at a right angle to your hips. This allows your center of mass to apply the most efficient amount of pressure to the wall keeping you in good contact. Placing your feet above or below your hips leads to slips and/or tipping over to your side and losing foot contact.

If you follow the above guidelines you should be good to go. I've seen lots and lots of needless falling on walls where adherence to the above tips would have allowed travel in a sprint.

Cargo Nets
An easy one, but still sweated by those a little leery of heights.

● Hand-over-hand on the vertical strands. Although the cargo net gives the appearance of a ladder, gripping the vertical strands gives you greater stability. Grasping the horizontal strands provides lots of slack as these are not the tied-in portions of the net.
● Foot-over-foot on the horizontal strands. Here you will utilize the ladder-like nature of the net.
● Keep your hips in. There is a tendency to sag your ass as you climb, this puts extra work on your arms. Standing upright and exaggerating a hips-in posture allows your legs to carry the weight and is a speedier, more efficient mode of cargo net travel.

CLIMBING

These events will have you climbing the wall, literally. Most of the walls are in the 4 to 6-foot range and well within the grasp of your standard fit human being. It's those 8 and 10-foot suckers and beyond that can bring most paces to an absolute stand still.

The good news is that most of the high walls have a step or hand-hold along the side for those who can't tackle the wall straight on. There's no shame in admitting you haven't mastered the vertical jump or upper-body hoisting yet. The other bit of good news is that if you utilize teamwork, a helping hand (or shoulder) will give you the up and over boost you need. Let's get some technique under our muddy belts so we can tackle these on our own.

Place foot with care. High walls are often approached by the uber-athlete with good speed and a foot placed about hip to chest high to assist on the initial reach. This is a sort of run into the wall and then up motion. And an excellent tactic in dry conditions — but your shoes are going to be muddy.

I have seen more than one competitor place that foot only to have it immediately slide askew leading to a less than cool head-on collision with the wall. Most of these collisions have been of the bump and bruise variety, but one led to some pretty impressive scalp bleeding, and that image has stayed with me. I switched to a jump and reach after that day.

I'm not saying you can't use the foot on the wall jump up — just saying be careful.

GOING UP

Jump up and elbow lever

I use this to clear walls from 6-10 feet. Stand at the base of the wall (you don't have to stop your stride if you choose, just make sure you jump more up than in or your knees will crack into that wall). Jump as high as you can, reaching for the top of the wall with both hands. As soon as your grip catches, aggressively pull up until you can hit an elbow lever position.

Once you hit your elbow lever you have two ways to mount. That is, to get on top of the wall.

See page 121 for elbow hitch pull ups — an exercise designed to develop elbow lever strength and technique.

Muscle-up

From your elbow lever position, lean into the wall so that your chest is on it. Aggressively hit a quasi-bar dip position bringing yourself to arms extended.

See page 120 for kip pull-ups — great for developing the upper body.

See page 122 for hot lava pull-ups — an excellent exercise to improve mounting and monkey traveling technique.

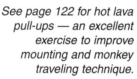

Heel hitch

From your elbow lever position, swing your leg (on the elbow lever side) up and hook your heel or the inside of your knee on top of the wall.

Using either method you will find, with work, that you will be able to coordinate all three steps — jump, elbow lever and muscle-up or heel hitch — into one smooth motion.

Now that we're on top of the wall, let's talk dismounts.

COMING DOWN
We've got three ways to go here.

1. Sight & drop
● The easiest of the dismounts if a little slow.
● Cross over to the other side of the wall and hang in the bottom of a pull-up position.
● Sight your landing (look before you leap).
● Let go and land with good form.

2. Prop vault

A speedy way to cross over the top, but perhaps iffy as the transition from mount to dismount is made so rapidly you may not have time to do a proper landing evaluation.

● From the top of the wall, position yourself on the palms of both hands and the sole of the heel hitch foot on the wall.

● Sight your landing and pass the unhitched foot underneath the hitched leg.

● Land with proper form.

The prop vault can be trained to become one smooth continuous motion, however that just may be its deficit as you may become so proficiently smooth that you deaden the tendency to stop and sight. But if you've got the smarts to remember to assess landings even when wet, muddy and exhausted, go for it.

3. Hip circle

Another speedy way to cross becomes one smooth motion and has the benefit of allowing for landing assessment. The drawback — the head-down position — worries some folks. But I use the hip circle almost exclusively and have never had a problem with it.

I will describe how to hit the hip circle with your body passing to your left in this sequence.

● From the top of the wall, grip the top of the wall with your right hand — fingers pointing behind you.
● Lean your head and chest down toward your landing and place your left palm on the wall approximately 2-3 feet down the wall.
● Sight your landing. Pulling with your top hand and pushing with your bottom hand, allow your hips to roll your legs over the wall.
● As your feet and knees come even with your bottom hand, release the wall with your top hand and stick a proper landing.

Again, the first method, while the slowest, is the surest for newbies. The second two are faster and require a bit more athleticism, but it's well worth working toward both.

CRAWLING LIKE A PRO

Often there will be yards and yards of barbed wire strung 15-20 inches off the ground. There may also be cramped tunnels that go on forever where it's just you in a dark teensy hole. Or surprisingly heavy water-logged tarps spread end-to-end for a very long ways that you've got to crawl under. No matter the height of the crawl, it's best to have a little form because, believe it or not, extended crawls in cold, wet mud with fire hoses blasting get to be mighty exhausting.

Bear crawl

If you are fortunate enough to have a low obstacle that will permit this half-crouch form of travel, let's do it with some skill. Raise the butt high and toward your feet so that your arms carry only a fraction of the load.

You can actually get some good speed out of a bear crawl if you put some practice into it.

Hands-and-knees crawl

Guess what this one is. Yeah, you know what to do.

Often long crawls are so low that neither the bear or hands-and-knees crawls will work. If you are permitted, you can log roll. Some events won't permit log rolling because it's an easier form of travel than belly crawling, and who wants to get off easy?

Log roll

Lying horizontally (how else?) extend your arms above your head as you roll.

Rocky terrain will often prompt us to pull our arms into our chest to protect our vitals, but...
● Our arms then become speed bumps for us to roll over, thus increasing our work.
● Arms-in also increases our body's circumference height and if that barbed wire is strung low you will catch a barb as each shoulder rolls through.

Belly crawl

When your obstacle is too low for the bear or hands-and-knees crawls and log rolling is not permitted or inadvisable, it's time to get all storming the beaches at Normandy low and hit the belly crawl.

● From a prone position, travel head first.

● You will be pulling yourself along on the bottom and outside edges of your forearms. The inside of the elbow is tender so it's best not to grind too much skin off it in the unkind terrain.

● To assist your forward momentum, time a push with one of your legs. The inside blade of the foot will be the point of contact with the ground.

One more thing about the belly crawl. Often you will be crawling a long, long way and this can get surprisingly tiring. You might find the following of value.

Dead-legging it

Use your elbow/forearm travel and one leg to propel you forward while you drag the other leg as if it were deadweight. Once your working leg becomes fatigued, switch off with the dead-leg. We have found this to be quite helpful in preserving and conserving energy on long low travels and have, para-doxically, increased our belly-crawl speed.

Going under

Often there will be low walls or obstructions that call for a quick drop to the ground to pass. Two ways to go.

Pivot bear

Here you will drop into bear crawl form, but ...
● Stack most of your weight over your hands as opposed to over your feet.
● Side step your legs under the obstacle to the other side.

Diving log roll
Very much what it sounds like.

CHECK THAT BALANCE

Occasionally you will have the opportunity to test your inner ear by traveling on top of a horizontal boom or beam.

Three ways to play it here.

Karl Wallenda

● Simply walk across it like a tight rope.
● Put your arms out for balance.
● Don't look at your feet, look at where you want to go.

Don't sweat not looking at your feet, your peripheral will do its job.

Cat walk

If the height is a little more than you like …
● Cross on your hands and feet — head first.
● Grip the surface with your hands as you travel.
● Keep your back parallel to the traveling surface — raising the hips higher raises your center of mass and can lead to toppling over.
● Travel hand-over-hand, foot-over-foot.

Crotch shuffle

If the height still has you worried, you can use this slow, awkward technique (slow and awkward, but it gets the job done.)

● Straddle the traveling surface facing the direction of travel.
● Lean forward onto your hands placing the majority of your weight on them.
● Shuffle your hips toward your hands.
● Reach forward with your hands and repeat.

Top secret grip tip

There's lots of climbing, folks. There's also gonna be lots of wet muddy conditions.

Put these two facts together, and we might come to the realization that wet, muddy hands might not be the best climbing option. Wiping your hands on your wet clothes won't cut it.

Here's what I suggest:
Any time you exit a water or mud hazard, pause at the side of the trail and wipe your hands thoroughly on nearby vegetation (grass or tree bark) or give them a sand rinse if dry sandy soil is nearby. Your hands will not be completely mud-free or dry, so after your trail-side ablutions, hit your run with your hands open, palms facing forward to allow the remaining water to

dry off and the mud to dry up. There is a tendency to close the fist when running, even closing it loosely stalls the drying process.

When you get to your next climbing obstacle, give them another veggie wipe or sand rinse and you should be good to go.

MONKEY BARS,
horizontal ladders,
booms and traverse walls

Often there will be rigid structures for you to scale or traverse. These can be made of lumber, metal or stacked cargo containers. Heck, I've encountered stacked junked cars and surprisingly hard to scale walls of hay bales. Because it's tough to prepare specifically for such variety, I offer the following general tips to assist.

When you must scale or traverse a structure where your hand holds are overhead, you can sample one of these three varieties.

Hand-over-hand

This works very well on booms or horizontal ladders. It's just what it sounds like. I suggest going for smooth speed over a stop-and-pause tempo. Stopping and resting between reaches will burn up the grip.

Side-slip

On a narrow boom you can hand-over-hand or side-slip. To side-slip, one shoulder faces the direction of travel the entire way. Reach first the lead hand forward then bring the rear hand up to it.

Rinse, wash, repeat.

I find the side-slip more efficient than the hand-over-hand since the latter causes the body to swing with each reach and overloads the grip.

Monkey Travel

For longer boom or monkey bar travels you might want to save that grip and opt for the monkey travel, which is the same thing we use on a horizontal rope.

No

Since your climbing surfaces and construction may vary, feel free to mix and match technique. That is, adapt and improvise as circumstances demand.

Traverse Walls

These are basically homemade bouldering walls approximately 16-20 feet long. You are provided with hand and footholds that protrude 2 inches from the wall. Your job is to cross the wall from right to left without falling off. No worries about he fall, you're never more than a couple of feet off the ground at any given time.

The following tips should help you on the traverse wall and can be adapted to more serious climbs.

● Grab with the whole hand if possible and not simply grip your handhold. Use friction and surface area to "stick" you to your handhold rather than just pinch gripping the stubs.
● The more foot the better. Try and get the a maximum amount of foot onto your footholds and not simply tip-toe across. Again, surface area is your friend.
● Hips in. Keep your hips as obscenely close to the wall as you can. This will reduce the weight on your grip, placing more weight on your legs, which are used to carry the load. Going hips out pulls you off the wall.
● Don't forget to pull and push. There is often a tendency to simply pull or step yourself across the wall. You will find pushing or wedging your body between transitions is a wiser way to go. Don't be afraid to be creative.

No

CARRY THAT LOAD

You may be required to hoist, lug or drag a heavy cumbersome object for some distance and perhaps over and under some less than fun terrain. Beyond simply having the strength to manage such tasks, which we'll help you build in the training section, there are a few general tips I can pass along.

Center the load over your hips

If you can get your object onto a shoulder and find a good balancing point, excellent. If it is a soft object such as a sandbag, I've had success placing it on top of my head water-bearer style.

Take shorter steps

If you're a strong athlete, there is a tendency to sprint these carries. But I've seen big men, who no doubt had the guns to move this load, gas out going up a long hill. Shorten you stride and concentrate on balancing the load.

Lift with the legs.

No

Hip-in

If the object is too large to get to your shoulder or too hard for your head, clutch it high on your chest and arch your hips forward to help center the load.

Tossing that weight

Use your legs to launch the weight.

Stick that drag chain to you

If your task is to drag a heavy object with a chain or rope attached to it, don't simply grip the chain in one or both hands and start hauling. This will burn the grip out and relies too much on the arms and shoulders. Instead ...

Plaster that lead to your hip or over your shoulder (if the lead is long enough). Here your grip is used to keep the lead in place against your body while your body does the hauling — not your arms.

... always ask yourself, "Can I adapt or innovate here to be better?"

Conditioning

Let's see now, we need to know what sort of event to expect. Have we discussed that? *Check.*

A little background on the genesis of obstacle courses would be nice. *Check.*

A little how-to strategy, tips and tactics to better see us through what we might be unfamiliar with. *Check.*

Is there gas in the tank, the muscle in the guns, the grit in the character to see the job done? Let's start that conversation right now.

We first discuss some general principles used to justify some of the madness you will encounter in this section. Second, we offer several specific workout templates or menus that you can use to get from 0 to 80 in your conditioning in minimum time. Notice I didn't say minimum effort.

Once you start using the conditioning menus, feel free to work through them in a linear fashion and when reaching the end, simply start the cycle again attempting to match or beat prior times and/or poundage.

Or if you prefer constant variability in training (as we all should and I'll explain shortly), head over to our website www.extremeselfprotection.com and click the inTENS tab. It provides info on six brand-spanking new workout templates that can be sent to your inbox each and every week.

Nature is not so smooth

"Nature is not smooth" is a little nugget of wisdom from the premier philosopher of randomness, Nassim Nicholas Taleb. Taleb applies this axiom across many disciplines and uses this observation to deconstruct assumptions regarding financial markets, top-down policy "solutions" and computer models, among

> ... man evolved and adapted to a world far more random, far more dangerous and far more variable than the one most of us inhabit today.

many other endeavors of spurious human prediction. He has briefly digressed on nature's "roughness" vs. the "smoothness" of gyms, and it is this observation that I want to expand upon as I see it holding huge implications for how we approach our conditioning for obstacle courses, which by their very nature are unpredictable animals themselves.

In a nutshell, Taleb's axiom is an evolutionary perspective on how the human body and mind developed. If we take this long view, we must allow that man evolved and adapted to a world far more random, far more dangerous and far more variable than the one most of us inhabit today. A world where food was pursued with actual cunning and physical work and run down in terrains and conditions that never exactly duplicated previous hunts. A world where the "knowable" was a bit less certain (the path home may always lead to home, but the potential for diversion/interruption may be more dire than a spot of traffic). A world where the sprints may not be of "regulation" distance, the loads not necessarily equally distributed or easily grasped, the work-to-rest intervals not precisely measured, the thermostat not adjusted just so before effort is exerted, the tasty protein bar not consumed before the task that "requires" it and so on and so on.

These observations should be of no real surprise to anyone steeped in evolutionary history. There have been moves made toward moving the dial from the smoothness of gyms toward the roughness of nature with any of the somewhat randomized conditioning regimens that alter tasks on a daily basis such as the CrossFit model. These efforts are a significant move in the right direction, but if we embody the full spirit of the axiom, we must recognize that further moves in the direction of roughing up our training can be made.

The current efforts at randomization, excellent as they are, still lean heavily on predictability/smoothness. The runs/sprints are measured distances culled from smooth sports, the lifts (for the most part) are two handfuls of smooth lifts, the calisthenics are dictated by smooth sport standards and performed on (or with) industry standard equipment (similar circumference pull-up bars and the like). Do not see this as an indictment of this approach — far from it. In the current environment, the randomized smooth sports being mixed and matched are head-and-shoulders above most dictated approaches. But the logic of the axiom demands a further push to roughing up the game. Assuming we are on board for an evolutionary/randomized perspective and the view that adapting training and diet closer to the circumstances under which this species evolved, then it's not much of a stretch to see that the move toward roughing may have some merit to it. Just as we see gains made by randomizing exercise circuits and mixing running/sprint intensity with lifting intensity, it is surmised that we may see even greater gains if we occasionally rough or randomize within the standard routines. We can do this by making all or the majority of our runs/sprints not on tracks, paths or treadmills, but off trail, up and down hills and over, under and through a variety of urban environments.

We can lift unwieldy objects or we can rough our gear by increasing bar circumference occasionally, experimenting with uneven grip positioning or uneven loading of the bar (it doesn't take much to throw your lifting form off, so approach in increments). We can decide to exercise outdoors more often than not. We can experiment with conditioning at different times of the day, with eating before the workout, three hours before or not at all that day. We can wear thick winter gloves when performing pull-ups, we can narrow our stance on squats to decrease balance. We can strive to alter terrain (simply jumping rope on gravel alters that task, for example). If you workout to music, try the occasional switch to music completely outside your taste to see how or if something as simple as that affects your performance. The potentials for variability seem limitless.

It is with this eye on constant variability that we will inform our conditioning. By rouging the gear and rouging the routines, you will find a tendency to focus less on questions such as "What do you bench?" or "How fast is your mile?" How do you answer these when your last bench was 240 pounds, 15 pounds of that loaded asymmetrically and the time before that your bench was only your bodyweight, but one foot was allowed on the floor and the other was held

... we may see even greater gains if we occasionally rough or randomize within the standard routines.

awkwardly in the air? Or your last mile was run holding a 45-pound plate alternately in the right and left hand, but never both hands at once or the mile before that was run in dress shoes?

When we rough the gear, rough the routine, the game becomes less about how well your times or lifts match or beat previous smooth iterations, but more along the lines of how much intensity can you bring to the roughed task at hand. If roughing the diet by moving toward paleo works for those who experiment with it (and quality research seems to support this assertion) and randomized conditioning seems to deliver greater results than adherence to smooth dogma, then it seems reasonable that the occasional introduction of roughness to smooth approaches, at least a few times per week, may potentially elicit similar gains.

A FEW ROUGH RULES

1. Train outside whenever possible. Yes, I know that you can't take all gear outside, but some can go with you (kettlebells, a weight plate or two) and some can be improvised (ledges or branches for pull-ups, for instance).

2. Variability is key. If the courses are never the same, why should our workouts be familiar? Yes, there are standard elements and events common to most courses, but invariably these elements are mixed-and-matched in different sequences, placed at different intervals and so on. Every foot

Quality study after quality study demonstrates that when it comes to conditioning, you get the most bang for your buck if you go for broke.

placement as you run through a ravine filled with unsteady rock must be carefully considered, not so with the usual run on a track, through a neighborhood or on a treadmill. Your brain can go on autopilot with these smooth predictable runs. Let variability put our heads back in the game.

3. Move effectiveness and efficiency to the top of your standards chart. It is common to benchmark our progress with two metrics, "How fast?" and/or "How heavy?" as in "What's your best 5K time?" or "What do you bench?" I'm not telling you to throw these metrics away since they provide some quantitative value, but I urge you to start considering the quality and or effectiveness of your movement as you confront training tasks. Sure, perform the tasks as quickly as you can, lift as heavy as you can, but please also keep an eye on quality and efficiency. Assess the somewhat intangible nature of movement quality and always ask yourself, "Can I adapt or innovate here to be better?"

4. Intensity. Quality study after quality study demonstrates that when it comes to conditioning, you get the most bang for your buck if you go for broke. That is, all-out sprints provide just as much (in some studies more) aerobic improvement and fat loss as longer runs (in some cases very long runs) of lesser intensity. A few high intensity lifts of heavy weights beats hands-down lots and lots of reps with lesser weight.

In busy lives where training time is limited, this is great news as it means we can get more done in less time. The bad news is that the intensity we are discussing is serious boundary pushing stuff. More good news — intensity is scalable, meaning what's a fast sprint to me may be a trot to you or what might be a heavy thruster to you might be a cakewalk to me.

Your job as the owner of your own bad self is to find your own redline and work to that threshold and not anyone else's. That will give you the improvements you need. For all the scientific skinny on intensity, see the aforementioned resources.

5. Intervals or matched distance. When it comes to these events there are two schools of thought regarding running. One is, "If the event is three miles

long, make sure you can run three miles." Makes mucho
sense when you hear it, but how does this jibe with
the research on intensity that seems to support intervals being equal to or superior to long distance training
in their conditioning effect?

Still confused? Here's the good news — these courses
are all intervals. Sure, a particular course may be three
miles long, but that three miles is broken up into intervals by obstacles. These events are not straight running
events, they are intervals (albeit some intervals are
longer than others) punctuated by tasks that have
nothing to do with running. So with the intensity/
interval research in mind and the fact that these
courses are all intervals, our training will reflect the
"it's all intervals" approach for the most part.

If you just love to run long distance, don't let me stand
in your way. Add inches, yards or miles to the distances
prescribed in the menus. Run to your heart's content,
all you die-hard runners. Everyone else, rest assured,
intervals will save you some time.

6. Suggestions and scalability. All the workouts
offered in the menu section will list suggested
poundage for weights, distances for running and repetitions for calisthenics. When you encounter numbers
inside parentheses, the first number is the prescription
for a fit athlete who's been training for some time, the
second for your weekend or progressing athlete and
the third is for the rookie.

But these are all just suggestions. Scale the numbers
even lower if your current condition will not allow you

to complete the day's task. Scale upward if you are some advanced cyborg who sweats not a drop at a weight and/or interval distance that would render most in need of a defibrillator.

> *Remember the phrase "Adapt and Improve." Don't be afraid to do just that.*

I'm providing suggestions here, you're your own boss. Remember the phrase "Adapt and Improve." Don't be afraid to do just that.

Exercises

I'm going to insult your intelligence and give a brief rundown of each exercise used in the menus. I want to make sure that we're all on the same page about form.

We also provide video demonstrations of some of these (and many more) on our *YouTube* channel *Hatmaker Combat Sports.*

Burpees

You gotta have these under your belt.

● Squat down placing your palms on the ground.

● Shoot your legs behind you into a push-up/plank position.

● Lower for one push-up (chest and upper thighs hitting the mat, no cheating by dropping the head or barely bending the arms).

● Shoot your legs back to a squat.

● Jump approximately 6-8 inches off the ground clapping your hands overhead.

Prisoner squats

● Place your hands behind your head.

● Keeping your torso erect, hit a deep squat.

● Stand up fully straightening the legs and pushing the hips forward.

Prisoner jump squats

● Performed like before but here you hit a 6 to 8-inch jump at the top of the motion.

Traveling prisoner jump squats

● Perform as you would a prisoner squat, but here you jump forward landing in your deep squat position.

● You may rebound as quickly as possible as long as you follow deep squat and hands-behind-head form.

Box jumps

- Using a 24-inch plyo-box, jump from the ground to the top of the box.
- Upon landing, stand up completely as you would at the top of a prisoner squat.
- Step to the ground — no rebounding.
- Repeat for the prescribed reps.

Dumbbell step-ups

● Using the 24-inch box, grip two dumbbells of prescription weight.

● Place one foot on top of the box and step up onto the box bringing both feet together into a complete standing position.

● Step down and repeat with the other leg.

● That's one rep.

Pull-ups (strict)

● From a full dead-hang ...
● Pull your chin above the bar.
● Rinse, wash, repeat.

Pull-ups (kip)

● From a full dead-hang ...
● Get that chin above the bar with any sort of kip,
hip-pop, ratcheting, wiggling that works for you.

Elbow hitch pull-ups

A mighty functional way to hit your pull-ups preparing you for wall mounting mechanics.

● From your dead-hang, use a powerful surge to get yourself above the bar so that you can ...

● Throw one of your elbows over the top catching and stopping yourself perched on an armpit.

Hot lava pull-ups

Another functional movement preparing you for overhead obstacles such as monkey bars.

● While doing your prescribed reps, anytime you feel the need to come off the bar hit either …
● An elbow hitch or a leg hook position.
● If you come off the bar, hit the penalty described in that menu's workout.

Chin-ups

● Think of a chin-up as a pull-up with your hands taking an undergrip on the bar.

● Use the mechanics of the pull-up.

Thrusters (dumbbell or barbell)

● Grip your weight in both hands.

● Squat until your thighs are just below parallel (we use a large medicine ball to keep our depth honest).

● With a ballistic rise, "thrust" the weights overhead to full-extension.

● Hit a brief pause at the top as proof of lift (POL).

Deadlift

We won't be deadlifting anywhere near power athlete territory, but this is an essential movement all the same.

- Take either an overgrip on the bar or an alternating grip (one over, one under).
- Keep your back flat and core tight.
- Stand lifting the bar to your knees.

Power cleans

This is a great movement to educate the explosive-ness vital for efficient tire flipping without actually having access to a huge tire.

● Take an overgrip on the bar.
● In one smooth explosive motion, clean the bar
(take the bar) to shoulder height.

Back squats

Another essential strength movement.

- First of all, a big smile because it's so much fun!
- Place the bar across your shoulders on your back.
- Keep your core tight and your back flat.
- Squat down until your thighs are just below parallel.
- Power back to a standing position.

Farmers walk

● Grip the prescribed dumbbell in each hand.
● Take them for a walk (not trot) for the designated distance.

Ball slams

A slam ball is a medicine ball that can take abuse. Sometimes we will toss it and fling it, but when the menu simply reads "slam ball"...

● Squat to the ball (don't bend over to it).
● Pick it up to your chest.
● Stand up thrusting the ball overhead.
● Squat in a ballistic manner slamming the ball to the ground.

Sandbag kongs

You can use a sandbag, an old heavy bag, large rocks, cinder blocks — whatever's available.

● Grip the object.
● Clean it to your shoulder.
● Press it overhead.
● Toss ● Repeat.

Hurdle hops

- Stand at a right angle to a hurdle.
- Jump laterally over the hurdle and immediately rebound back.
- Right and left is one repetition.

CONDITIONING MENUS

Each menu is a suggested single day of training. Some workouts may take no more than 5-10 minutes, others much longer (variability, remember?). The key to all of them is intensity — redline them all!

As for how many days per week to train — aim for three at a minimum while intermediate to advanced athletes may find more success with a three days on, one day off schedule. But you're the boss of you.

Where you see numbers separated by "/" the first number is a suggested poundage or repetition for advanced athletes, the second for intermediate athletes and the third for the rookies. Scale up or down to suit, but don't cheat the intensity.

I suggest working the menus straight through to kill your tendency to cherry pick and possibly play to your strengths. Let the variability and randomness work their magic.

Once you've worked through all of the templates (66 in all), start again at the beginning attempting to match or beat previous poundage and/or workout times or ...

Head over to our website at
www.extremeselfprotection.com
and click the inTENS tab. There you will find info on how to receive six new workouts every week of the year.

1
Burpees 100/75/50

2
Prisoner squats 25
Sprint 50 yards
X's 5 (rest one minute between rounds)

3
Travel 2 miles
At the top of each minute, alternate between running and bear crawling.

4
Burpees 10
Sprint 100 yards
X's 10/8/5

5
Tire drag 30 yards
Push-ups 10
X's 10/8/5
Drag any other suitable object such as a tire, log or cinder block.

6
Travelling prisoner jump squats 100 yards (uphill if possible)
Walk back and repeat
X's 5/4/3

7
Box jumps (24") 100/75/50

8
Run 2 miles
All "long" runs should be conducted outside and with as widely varied terrain as you can manage.

9
100 yard sprints X's 10 (30 seconds rest between)

10
Burpees 150/100/75

11
Pull-ups 100/100/75
Advanced must use strict pull-up form. Intermediate and rookies
can kip or wiggle up to the bar to their heart's content.

12
Dumbbell thrusters (50/40/30) 50

13
Run 2.5 miles

14
Burpees 100/75/50

15
Rope climb (15-20' rope) 10/8/6
If you find yourself unable to climb, grip the rope and attempt a
pull-up until you can apply blade-to-blade pressure to support
yourself. Allow six of these make-do's for each prescribed climb.

16
Slam ball (40/30/20)
Granny toss 50 yards
Slam ball carry 50 yards
X's 10
You will throw, toss, fling the slam ball any way you choose for
maximum distance. Continue until you hit your 50 yard mark,
then pick it up and sprint back to the beginning.

17
Farmer's walk (50/40/30) 50 yards
Run 1/10th mile
X's 10

18
Run 2.5 miles

19
Barbell thrusters (135/115/95) 3
Sprint 50 yards
Push-ups 10
Sprint back 50 yards
X's 10

20
Prisoner squats 20
One-arm dumbbell thruster — right arm (50/40/30) 5
Prisoner squats 20
One-arm dumbbell thruster — left arm (50/40/30) 5
X's 5

21
Run 3 Miles

22
Barbell thrusters (135/115/95) 50

23
Push-ups 10
Slam ball (40/30/20) 10
X's 10

24
Chin-ups 10/10/8
Advanced athletes will hit strict form, all others may kip and or wiggle as they see fit.
Low hurdle hops (right and left is one rep) 20
X's 10

25
Burpees 10/8/6
Standing broad jumps for 50/40/30 yards
X's 10
Use the broad jump to travel your distance — you must take off and land from and onto both feet.

26
Prisoner squats 10
Slam ball (40/30/20) 10
Burpees 10
X's 10

27
Chin-ups (strict) 5
One-arm dumbbell thrusters — right arm (50/40/30) 5
Jumping prisoner squats 15/12/10
One-arm dumbbell thrusters — left arm 5
Jumping prisoner squats 15/12/10
X's 10

28
Sprint 1/10th mile
Rest one minute
X's 10

29
Barbell thrusters (135/115/95) 10
Travelling prisoner jump squats 25 yards
Sprint back 25 yards
Countdown the thrusters from 10, as in 10 reps then 9, then 8,
et cetera.

30
Deadlift (225/200/185) 10
Bear crawl out 25 yards
Burpees 10
Bear crawl back 25 yards
Countdown the deadlift and burpees

31
Run 1.5 miles
Box jumps 100/75/50
Prisoner squats 100/75/50
Grieve for your legs.

32
Grab a kettlebell, dumbbell or sandbag and take it for an awkward, all-terrain 2-mile hike. (50/40/30)
Go over and around as many obstacles as you can manage.

33
Run your fastest mile but ...
At the top of each minute hit 25 prisoner jump squats

34
Back squat (bodweight/25 pounds under your BW/50 pounds under) 10
Bear crawl 50 yards
X's 5
If you drink, have a double on me.

35
100 pull-ups as follows:
The first 30 with 25/15/10 pounds hanging off your belt.
The next 30 strict, dead hang, no kip.
The next 30 kip (the kip is mandatory — no kip, don't count the rep).
The last 10 are elbow-hitch pull-ups.
Lay down a crash pad and enjoy the failures.

36
Run 2 miles
Use a varied terrain.

37
Run 1.5 miles with the following protocol:
Sprint at 90 percent effort for the first 15 seconds of each minute. Run at a reserve pace for the remaining 45 seconds of each minute.

38
100 Hot lava pull-ups
Each time you leave the bar, sprint 25 yards, hit 10 push-ups, sprint back and get on the bar immediately.

39
Sprint 30 seconds max effort
Rest 90 seconds
X's 5

40
Dumbbell step-ups (hold a pair of 25/15/10 DBs and step onto a
24" box) 8 per leg
24" Hurdle 8
X's 8

41
Run 2 miles

42
Kettlebell swing (70/50/40) 150

43
Run your fastest mile

44
Jump over 24" hurdle 100/80/60

45
Slam ball toss travel (40/3020) 1 mile
Toss the ball any way you choose, walk or run to it, repeat until
your distance is covered.

46
Standing broad jumps (make your jump distance your height)
10
Back squats (135/115/95) 10
X's 10

47
Run your fastest mile

48
Chin-Ups (strict) 100/75/50

49
Run 1/4 mile
Prisoner squats 50/40/30
X's 6

50
Pull-ups max, rest one minute and repeat for a total of three sets of maxes.
Then rope climb — three trips on a 20' rope

51
1/2 mile sprint
Rest one minute and repeat
Rest one more minute then grab a 45#/35#/25# weight and travel 1/4 mile

52
Prisoner squats 50/40/30
Pull-ups 10/8/6
Chin-ups 10/8/6
X's 10

53
Slam ball squat and jump launch (40/30/20) 100 yards
Slam ball carry 1/2 mile
Slam ball squat and jump launch protocol: Clean the ball, hit a full deep squat, jump as high as you can and push pass the ball as far as you can at the top of the jump. Run to the ball and repeat for the designated distance.

54
Strict pull-ups (no kip) 10
Travelling prisoner jump squats 20 yards
Countdown the pull-ups from 10

55
Hot lava pull-ups 100/75/50
Hit 10 burpees each time you come off the bar.

56
Sandbag kongs 75/50/30
Use a bag between 50-90 pounds — the heavier the better for
seasoned athletes.

57
Push-ups 150/125/100
Each time you hit failure (a knee hitting the mat) stand and hit
10 burpees.

58
Sprint 100 Yards
Bear crawl 50 Yards
X's 5

59
Kettlebell swings (70/50/40) 20
Pull-ups 20/15/10
Back-pedal 50 yards
X's 5

60
Maximum prisoner squats in 20 minutes.

61
Rope climb (20') 1
Back squat (bodyweight) 10
Count down the back squats from 10

62
Power clean (155/135/1155) 10
Prisoner squats 20
Count down the power cleans from 10

63
Prisoner squats 20
Toes to bar 10
X's 10

64
Farmer's walk 200 yards (50/40/30)
Box jumps 100/75/50

65
Power clean (135/115/95) 5
Push-ups 10
Prisoner squats 15
X's 15

66
Sprint 1/2 mile
Rest two minutes
X's 3

What to eat

Super secret high performance nutrition

Chances are since you are reading a book about physical activity, you already engage in some form of physical conditioning to bolster your sport performance. I would also wager that if you are serious about your training to any degree, you have some pretty specific ideas regarding nutritional intake. You might be a Paleo-enthusiast in one of its many forms or possibly you're still hanging on to the Zone or the South Beach Diet.

> *It's the work — not what you eat.*

Maybe you're an old schooler and an Atkins' proselytizer. Perhaps you're a low fat proponent. Or is it high fat? Do you go for the carbs and carbo load or adhere to the Okinawa protocol? The Mediterranean diet? Are you a strict vegetarian or an all-meat, grass-fed, I-shot-it-myself carnivore.

If I missed your particular take on fuel, I would still place a bet that it is a subdivision or variant of the above panoply. After all, there are only so many ways to juggle the proportions of the three primary constituents of nutrition — protein, carbohydrates and fat.

I will also wager that you've got some pretty good reasons for why you eat what you do and why those who don't follow the same path are a bit misled and not living up to their full potential. Forgive me if this estimation sounds a bit dismissive, but, let's face it, many of us place a lot of faith in the foods we eat imbuing them with qualities that seem to fall short of magical for the "good" foods and bad juju for the "no-no" foods. I've been there myself. I've been a vegan (in a variety of forms), a food-combiner, a low-carber, an all-meat guy, a this-er, a that-er, a fellow searcher who knew that if I

> ... what exactly is it that all of these top-performing athletes have in common? Well, the answer is hard qualitative work in high quantities.

got the dinner plate alchemy just right, I would be that much faster, this much stronger, have this much more endurance.

I could find proof for the success of each faith-based path of nutritional wisdom I aligned myself with at the time. I could point to good "science" that supported the belief du jour (while conveniently ignoring the null hypotheses). I could lean hard on my own anecdotal evidence of personal feelings about each awesome diet. I could point to performance numbers showing improvements in tasks and somehow downplay or ignore the idea that these improvements in performance had less to do with the actual training and more to do with what I chewed or what supplement I popped.

I will wager that my experience is shared by many of you. You've either been on this search for the "right thing" treadmill yourself or have personal experience with fellow athletes who pursue a variety of nutritional religions, which we all treat with short memories as soon as we become converted to the next true thing.

Like I said, I've been there, done that and have come to a simple, good news conclusion regarding the art of eating: It's the work — not what you eat.

Wanna eat a large cheese pizza? How about chocolate chip pancakes? Bowls of grits? Pasta? Pop-Tarts? Ben & Jerry's Cheesecake Brownie Ice Cream? How about beer? (Now that got your attention.)

These are just some of the foods that appeared on the menus of 2012 Olympic athletes. These are not off-season, out-of-training foods. These are truly Olympian food choices. Not food splurges or "cheat day" foods. These aren't even isolated "Oh, I had these four slices of French toast so I'd better not have anything else" foods. These are just some of the so-called "junk foods" that the best of the best consume in a 6,000 calorie day, look-at-me-I'm still-ripped-to-shreds-like-a-superhero regimen. Candy bars, cookies, pizza and beer. How's that for supplementation?

Sure, there are some Olympic athletes who consume their calories in ways that more resemble those listed in the opening paragraph — carefully measured "correct" foods. But what we've got to keep in mind is that those who eat "junk," those who eat "right," those who eat carbs, those who eat meat, those who eat according to whatever belief, all performed at levels beyond the expectations of the common person either because of or in spite of their food choices.

So what if it isn't necessarily what we chow down that's the magic formula? If it's not a one-size-fits-all elite nutrition program that is the secret to Olympic caliber performance or aesthetics, what exactly is it that all of these top-performing athletes have in common? Well, the answer is hard qualitative work in high quantities. And it is this fact of hard, hard grueling work that causes a lot of the magic food ideas to begin to take root.

Composing a shopping list and resisting a few no-no food items while sticking to those foods with good ju-ju is a far, far easier job than pushing the body to extremes. We are economical animals and look for easy/cheap solutions whenever and wherever possible, and there's no seemingly cheaper or easier answer to elite fitness than magic food. If I can get the magic potion just right, the menu tweaked just so, then I too can be golden.

Unfortunately, the evidence says this just isn't true. You can cast about for evidence to support practically any side of the performance nutrition morass and find reams of bolstering information. On the other hand you can find just as much evidence to tear down much of the positive support you can find for the view you wish to support.

These 6,000 calorie-a-day athletes, whether on so called junk food or healthy diets, put in enormous amounts of strenuous work. (I quibble with the word "junk" as it pertains to food. Tell a starving citizen of a third world nation that a Twinkie is garbage and a poor health choice, and then after that bit of cruelty, see if you can realign your priorities a bit). This prodigious amount of work supports a calories in/calories out model no matter the source of the calories. Those starving in some regions of the world are stark evidence that if you kill those calories, the weight comes off whether you want it to or not.

... as long as the work load is of high quality, we can be a bit less dogmatic about what we eat.

Let's face it, we aren't Olympic athletes and our workloads simply will not justify 6,000 calories per day no matter their source. But it seems that whether we use the models of Olympic consumption or our own anecdotal evidence of being on this diet or that diet and our body still doing what it does, as long as the work load is of high quality, we can be a bit less dogmatic about what we eat. We don't have to go candy shop crazy since we are not doing Olympic caliber work, but we do have more latitude about what we consume than many of us believe.

For weight control we've got two ways to go. We can adjust caloric intake up or down or we can adjust workload up or down. The optimum mix is to tweak both avenues simultaneously. For some, this info is going to be great news — it appears to allow hard-working athletes a longer leash in regard to food.

For some, this info may be bad news in two ways. It is possible to eat lots of so-called bad foods and still be a lean, mean, hard-charging athlete, but you gotta work

H-A-R-D to get away with it. You can't shortcut the work. Some will remain happier with the easier job of composing restrictive grocery shopping lists.

> *It is possible to eat lots of so-called bad foods and still be a lean, mean, hard-charging athlete, but you gotta work H-A-R-D to get away with it.*

The second way the info may be a bit of bad news is that if you are firmly committed to your "scientifically proven high-performance nutrition program" du jour, the cognitive dissonance may make eating whatever you damn well please as long as you are willing to do the work a bit hard to swallow.

I get that skepticism. Those immersed in physical training are (and always have been) confronted with conflicting fuel ideas every which way they turn. How could there not be something to it? I point again to Olympic diets whether deemed good, bad or indifferent, and again to the similarity of excellent results and see that the only commonality is eating enough calories to support your workload and then burn those calories off with ultra-high quality work.

Logistics

We've talked about all the exciting stuff, now let's spend a little time on logistics, the little details that make sure you have as smooth an experience as possible.

Gear
The following are only suggestions. Some love running shirtless or as near to naked as they can get. Look at the abrasions post-race on these brave folks and ask yourself, "Is this for me?" If so, strip down.

Or consider cold weather events. I've seen the skins crew rarin' to go at the beginning, but more often than not, they might be looking for an EMT or an ATV before long hoping for an emergency blanket ASAP.

Cold induced cramps halfway up a rope ain't no fun. You ever shiver until you fell on your face? I've seen it happen numerous times. Better cold and miserable than ridiculously cold and miserable I always say.

Some folks run these races in costumes — the more outrageous the better. If that's your thing, please keep it up, I love the variety. For the fuddy duddy, pragmatic-minded folks, pay attention to the following.

No cotton. Natural fibers do not wick. They slurp up all that water, all that heavy mud and add to the load you will be carrying throughout the course, over and under things, up and down hills and ropes. If this extra weight sounds fun, natural fibers it is.

For all others...

Synthetic fibers and/or cold-warm compression gear. Any of the clothing manufactured by Under Armor and other like brands are top choices. Shedding as much of that water and mud weight as you can is a good thing.

Don't go loose. Billowy shorts and or shirts (or costumes) will get caught on barbed wire, caught on walls, rocks and such. If you like going mandatory shirtless or hole-in-the-seat-of-your-britches at the midpoint, ignore this advice.

Long-sleeves and/or long tights. If your gear is long-sleeved and/or long-legged you'll have a crawling advantage. Long crawls and numerous crawls will incur lots of abrasions. Covering up those delicate elbows and knees can keep your epidermis relatively blemish and grit-free.

Gloves. Some inexpensive rubberized/water-resistant gloves can be of value to keep that grip for walls and rope. I wear them only for cold weather events, but to be honest I can't tell if there's much of an advantage over the long haul. So make of this advice what you may. I know some folks who cut the tips off the fingers of their gloves thus allowing water to drain. But this didn't work for me. If you plan on wearing gloves in your event, train in them to get used to the feel.

Gel packs. For any race six miles and up, I highly recommend packing a gel pack for each 3 mile increment. Not really necessary for the 3-4 mile courses, but around mile 6 that familiar bonk feeling hits. For longer races I find a gel pack at miles 6, 9 and 12 leaves me at the end feeling just as I do as if the event were only a 3-4 miler.

Carry your hydration?

All of these races urge you to pack water. I've never done this for two reasons. First, it's extra weight and something else to get caught on an obstacle. And second, I've never been in an event where there were not water stations plentifully positioned throughout.

Tips

I offer these so that your only obstacles are on the course and not due to inefficient planning.

● **Preregister.** You wanna save a little money and hassle, this is how you do it.

● **Wanna save more money?** Many of these events will offer packages; sign up for more than one event and you get deeper discounts. (Wait until you've run your first one to make sure it's your cup of muddy tea).

● **Wanna run for free?** Many of these events will barter with you. Volunteer to work the course or some aspect of the course for a day and you earn a free shot at the course.

● **Heat choices.** Some events will allow you to select specific heats (times to run) or run days (in two-day events). Your choices may depend on who you are.

● *Wanna skip hotel costs?* Position toward midday so you can drive in, run and drive back.

● *Wanna get the maximum out of the post-race party atmosphere?* Day one is prime.

● *Wanna thinner crowd and faster experience?* Doesn't always work, but I have found that by day two any bugs that may have been discovered in a course or the event-side logistics have been worked out making life a bit easier for all concerned.

● *Have your paperwork done.* If you were smart enough to preregister online, also be smart enough to have all your paperwork filled out ahead of time. You'd be surprised how many folks wait until they are at the front of a long line to behave like a senior citizen still writing checks at the grocery store. Don't be that guy or gal.

● *Have your paperwork and photo ID in hand.* You will need both. Again, holding up the line while you dig through an overstuffed backpack is less than polite. Man, do you guys annoy me. Get with the program.

● *Have a little cash available.* There will be a bag check (one bag). Sometimes you gotta pay for this (most often cash only). It can be a long walk to the parking lot, then out to find an ATM just to come back and start all over again.

● *Get there early*. Event rules will tell you to be there anywhere from an hour to 90 minutes early.

Take them seriously. Often parking is ridiculous and much of that reserve time is eaten up simply waiting in line. Some events will have you park, then shuttle you to the actual event location — obviously this adds even more travel time. I suggest that whatever time they suggest to be there, tack another half hour on to that for safety. (Even following this extra half-hour rule we have missed our heat by an hour in a shuttle wait. The event made good on a later heat that day, but be prepared).

● *Bib Placement.* Bibs are often ripped off in the race. Bibs placed high on the back will snag on barbed wire. Those placed low on the belly will eat it during a belly crawl. High on the chest seems to have best results, but even this is imperfect. Marking your bib number on your forehead seems to be the ideal way to stay tagged for event photos.

● *Ladies only (and our longer-haired fellers)* For those who have long hair, my wife suggests a high and tight pony tail to reduce hair being dragged through the mud and to keep those inevitably muddy tresses out of one's face.

● *Have fun, it's a party!* Don't take it seriously. Get out there and be all you can be, but job one is to have a blast!

Cleaning up

Now that all the muddy fun is over and you've celebrated, it's time to get clean and even that ain't all that easy. Here are a few tips to help expedite that gooey, muddy process.

First and foremost, realize that you are not coming clean at the race site. The best you can hope for is to look less like a fugitive than you currently do.

Take advantage of onsite water sources. If there are outside showers offered, rinse off. If there are fire hoses spritzing down post-race folks, hop in that cold spray. If there is an available natural water source that is not posted off limits and not being used as part of the course, dive in. Anything you can do to rinse at least some of the mud off will be a big help.

Pack a trash bag. When you change out of your filthy clothes, plopping your muddy clothes into a trash bag will save additional clean-up of your backpack, car trunk or whatever else might come into contact with your unbagged soiled wardrobe.

Pack a couple of towels. Towel number one is to wipe down after you've taken advantage of the water source. Towel two is to lay on your vehicle seats assuming you have a vehicle you deem worthy of protecting.

Wet wipes and Q-tips. These are optional as most of the major cleaning will be done at home. But if you'd like to wipe some of that red clay mud from your face, neck and arms before entering your local KFC for some post-race calories, wet wipes come in quite handy.

What to do with your shoes. Many people toss 'em. Lots of folks donate them to charity (seriously). But if you've got more racing in your future, save the investment and take them home.

Laundry. I recommend not dumping your trash bag directly into your washer when you get home. Instead, dump your clothes and shoes in the yard. Spread them out and hit them with the water hose with the pressure on high. Takes about 3-5 minutes to drive most of the mud out, then you can pop them into the machine (don't mix with your other clothes). If you do this, one time through the machine should do the trick.

Shower. When you first hit the shower, you will discover that you have far more crevices for mud to hide in than you thought humanly possible. Enjoy the search. I recommend using a dark colored rag and washcloth for your first shower because no matter how well you tend to your bathing hygiene, you will discover with a white towel that there's still a bit of squeaking to be done.

That's it

I hope you've both enjoyed and found a tip or two that you can use. If you have additional tips that you think would be of value, please send them my way for possible use in a future edition. Send them to mark@extremeselfprotection.com

In the meantime, get out there and have some muddy fun. And if you happen to see me at one of these events, please come over and introduce yourself. I'm always happy to meet a fellow big kid who enjoys playing in the mud.

Let's end this with wise words that most of us heard from our parents when we were kids, "For God's sake, get out of the house, go outside and play!"

Resources

The following are only a few of the events that are out there — these are some of the big dogs. There are lots of smaller local events popping up left and right, and I heartily encourage you to give those a shot as well. I've had some great times on courses engineered by a few folks with a limited budget but with lots of ingenuity.

www.extremeselfprotection.com

This is my website, not an event. Go to the inTENS page for more Obstacle Course Racing Conditioning Menus.

www.toughguy.co.uk/

The original and still the awesomenest. Do yourself a favor and check out the site for Mr. Mouse's words of wisdom. He's a class act.

www.spartanrace.com

www.warriordash.com

www.runforyourlives.com

Obstacle course racing with extra added zombies. What's not to love?

www.ruggedmaniac.com

www.mudathlon.com

www.rebelrace.com

www.goruckchallenge.com

While not strictly an obstacle course race, more of an experience, it is still mighty worthy to be included and well worth your time.

www.sqwishsqwashchallenges.com

www.toughmuddeer.com

www.mudandadventurecom

There are many listings of the large and small events out there, but I find this one pretty darn useful.

Tips from organizers

From the folks at Run for Your Lives, aka The Zombie Run

1. If this is your first race, start running a few weeks out to ensure you can complete the course. Also, practice short sprints.

2. Even if you've done 167 adventure races before, you still won't be prepared for what's coming. Incorporate dodging moves and maneuvers into your training.

3. Expect the unexpected.

4. Protect your flags.

5. Get ready to Run For Your Lives!

From the folks at Warrior Dash

1. Think your costume through.

2. Start training early.

3. Bring money for a turkey leg.

4. Bring friends. The more the merrier.

5. Try different venues. All our courses are different.

6. A bonus tip — Consider forming a team to raise money for the St. Jude's Warriors Connection. You can have fun and help at the same time.

A Tip from Max Villalobos of SquishSqwashchallenges

We're American made and Navy SEAL sponsored so our courses are more military minded. We're all about team camaraderie — no one is left behind on the course.

Tips from Rob Dickens of Rugged Maniac

1. Run, run, run.

2. Run in terrain with elevation.

3. Use trail running shoes — padded shoes get heavy when wet.

4. I recommend using athletic sleeves for elbows and knees.

Tips from Sophie Pollitt-Cohen of GoRuckChallenge

1. This is a team event, not a race. You will be led for 12 hours through an urban course by a Green Beret.

2. Think of your cadre (leader) as a resource, not a drill sergeant. Do not be afraid to ask questions.

3. When it's deep into the process, we call that the Witching Hour. Don't start bargaining with yourself, saying things such as "I'll quit if we go in the water again." Learn to dig deep.

4. Skip the minimal sole or glove toe-shoes. The cadre call them the Five-finger death punch.

5. Expect something different from us. We under promise and over deliver.

Index

*Videos by Mark Hatmaker
available through Paladin*

The ABCs of NHB
High-Speed Training for No Holds Barred Fighting

Beyond Brazilian Ju-jitsu
Redefining the State of the Art in Combat Grappling

Extreme Boxing
Hardcore Boxing for Self-Defense

The Floor Bag Workout
The Ultimate Solo Training for Grapplers and Groundfighters

Gladiator Conditioning
Fitness for the Modern Warrior (with companion workbook)

The Submission Encyclopedia
The Ultimate Guide to the Techniques and Tactics of Submission
Fighting

The Complete Grappler
The Definitive Guide to Fighting and Winning on the Ground
(with companion workbook)

Paladin Enterprises, Inc.
7077 Winchester Circle Boulder, CO 80301 303.443.7250
303.442.8741 fax
www.paladin-press.com

Titles by Mark Hatmaker
www.extremeselfprotection.com
At all major bookstores and e-booksellers

No Holds Barred Fighting:
The Ultimate Guide
to Submission Wrestling
The combat art of The Ultimate Fighting
Championships.
978-1-884654-17-6 / $12.95
695 photos

More No Holds Barred Fighting:
Killer Submissions
More takedowns, rides and submissions
from the authors of *No Holds Barred*
Fighting.
978-1-884654-18-3 / $12.95
650 photos

No Holds Barred Fighting:
Savage Strikes
The Complete Guide to Real World
Striking for NHB Competition
and Street Defense
Punches, kicks, forearm shots, head
butts and more.
978-1-884654-20-6 / $12.95
850 photos

Boxing Mastery
Advance Techniques, Tactics and Strategies from the Sweet Science
Advanced boxing skills and ring general-ship.
978-1-884654-29-9 / $12.95
900 photos

No Holds Barred Fighting:
Takedowns
Throws, Trips, Drops and Slams for NHB Competition and Street Defense
978-1-884654-25-1 / $12.95
850 photos

No Holds Barred Fighting:
The Clinch
Offensive and Defensive Concepts Inside NHB's Most Grueling Position
978-1-884654-27-5 / $12.95
750 photos

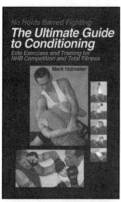

No Holds Barred Fighting:
The Ultimate Guide to Conditioning
Elite Exercises and Training for NHB
Competition and Total Fitness
978-1-884654-29-9 / $12.95
900 photos

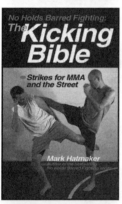

No Holds Barred Fighting:
The Kicking Bible
Strikes for MMA and the Street
978-1-884654-31-2 / $12.95
700 photos

No Second Chance:
A Reality-Based Guide to Self-Defense
How to avoid and survive an assault.
978-1-884654-32-9 / $12.95
500 photos

No Holds Barred Fighting:
The Book of Essential Submissions
How MMA champions gain their victories. A catalog of winning submissions.
978-1-884654-33-6 / $12.95
750 photos

MMA Mastery: Flow Chain Drilling
and Integrated O/D Training
to Submission Wrestling
Blends all aspects of the MMA fight game into devastating performances.
978-1-884654-38-1 / $13.95
800 photos

MMA Mastery: Ground and Pound
A comprehensive go-to guide — how to win on the ground.
978-1-884654-39-8 / $13.95
650 photos

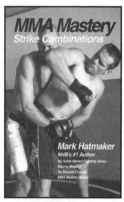

MMA Mastery: Strike Combinations
Learn the savage efficiency of striking in combinations. A comprehensive guide.
978-1-935937-22-7 / $12.95
1000 photos

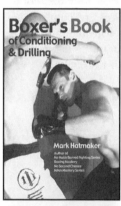

**Boxer's Book of
Conditioning & Drilling**
How to get fighting fit like the champions.
978-1-935937-28-9 / $12.95
650 photos

Boxer's Bible of Counterpunching
The Killer Responce to Any Attack
978-1-935937-47-0 / $12.95
500 photos

Mark Hatmaker is the bestselling author of the *No Holds Barred Fighting Series,* the *MMA Mastery Series, No Second Chance, Boxing Mastery, Boxer's Book of Conditioning & Drilling* and

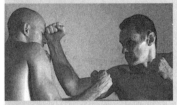

Boxer's Bible of Counterpunching. He also has produced more than 40 instructional videos. His resume includes extensive experience in the combat arts including boxing, wrestling, Jiu-jitsu and Muay Thai.

He is a highly regarded coach of professional and amateur fighters, law enforcement officials and security personnel. Hatmaker founded Extreme Self Protection (ESP), a research body that compiles, analyzes and teaches the most effective Western combat methods known. ESP holds numerous seminars throughout the country each year including the prestigious Karate College/Martial Arts Universities in Radford, Virginia. He lives in Knoxville, Tennessee.

www.extremeselfprotection.com

Doug Werner is author or coauthor of 20 sport instructional guides, including the bestselling *Start-Up Sports®* series. He lives in Chula Vista, California.

Our sport instructional guides are bestsellers because each book contains hundreds of images, is packed with expert advice and retails at a great price. No one else comes close.

trackspublishing.com